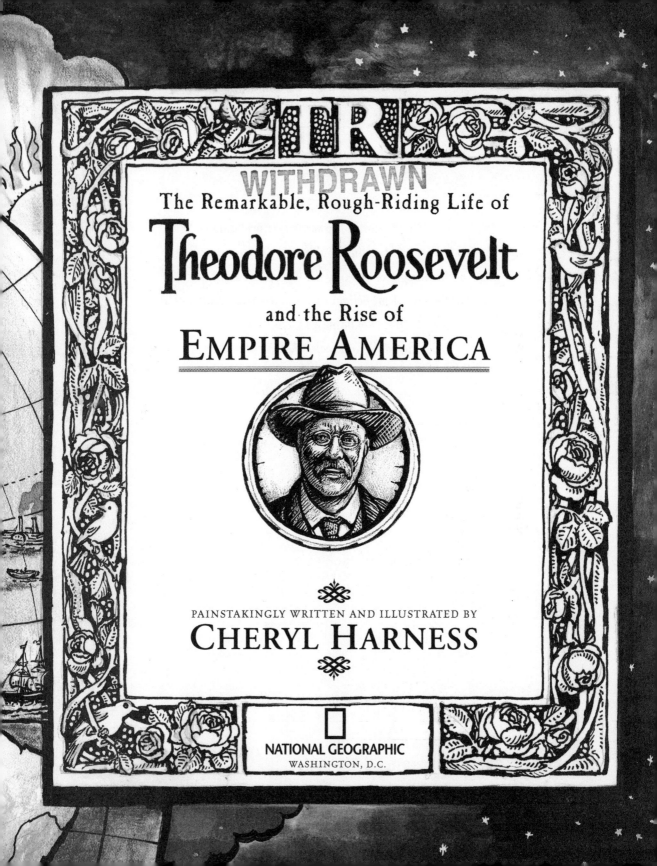

TR

The Remarkable, Rough-Riding Life of

Theodore Roosevelt

and the Rise of

EMPIRE AMERICA

PAINSTAKINGLY WRITTEN AND ILLUSTRATED BY

CHERYL HARNESS

NATIONAL GEOGRAPHIC

WASHINGTON, D.C.

"There must be the keenest sense of duty,
and with it must go the joy of living; there must be shame
at the thought of shirking the hard work of the world,
and at the same time delight in the many-sided beauty of life.
With soul of flame and temper of steel,
we must act as our coolest judgment bids us."

— Theodore Roosevelt
October 1, 1913

Contents

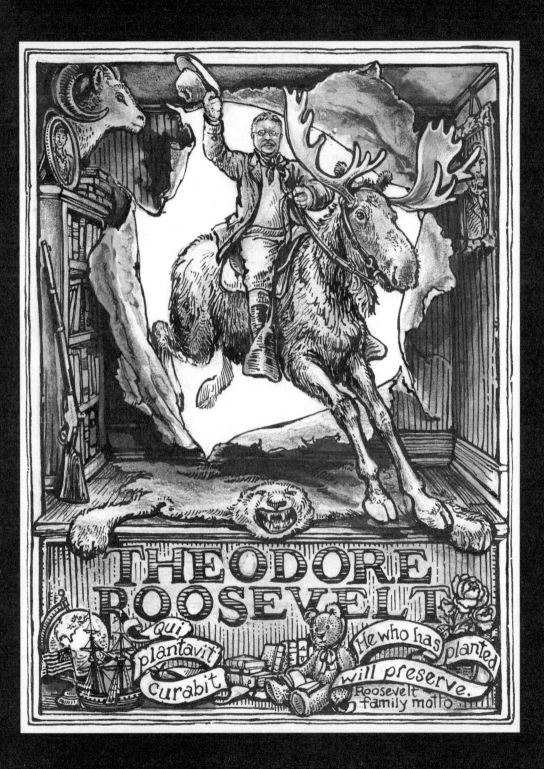

THEODORE ROOSEVELT

Qui plantavit curabit

He who has planted will preserve.
Roosevelt family motto

I F YOU EXAMINE A PARTICULAR PICTURE taken in New York City on April 25, 1865, you can just barely see six-year-old Theodore Roosevelt and his little brother Elliott. From a window in their grandfather's mansion, they're watching President Lincoln's funeral procession. For asthmatic, puny Theodore and his country, still reeling from years of Civil War, the next decades will be a time of amazing transformation.

When Theodore was a baby, letters written by candlelight might be carried by Pony Express. When he died, the sky hummed with electrical wires and airplanes. As the U.S. muscled its way out of its past to become a mighty nation, TR – as he'd be known – overcame illness and tragedy to become a powerful adventurer, America's youngest President, and one of its most interesting citizens ever. Sure, there were contradictions. TR was a peacemaker who gloried in war. He delighted in and tried to conserve the natural world, yet he blasted many a beast clear out of it. The nation based upon liberty and equality could be ruthless, bigoted, and greedy. Still, at the dawn of the 20th century, both man and nation set the scene for the world power we are these days. Learn about Theodore Roosevelt and his America, and you may decide that they were pretty much perfect for each other.

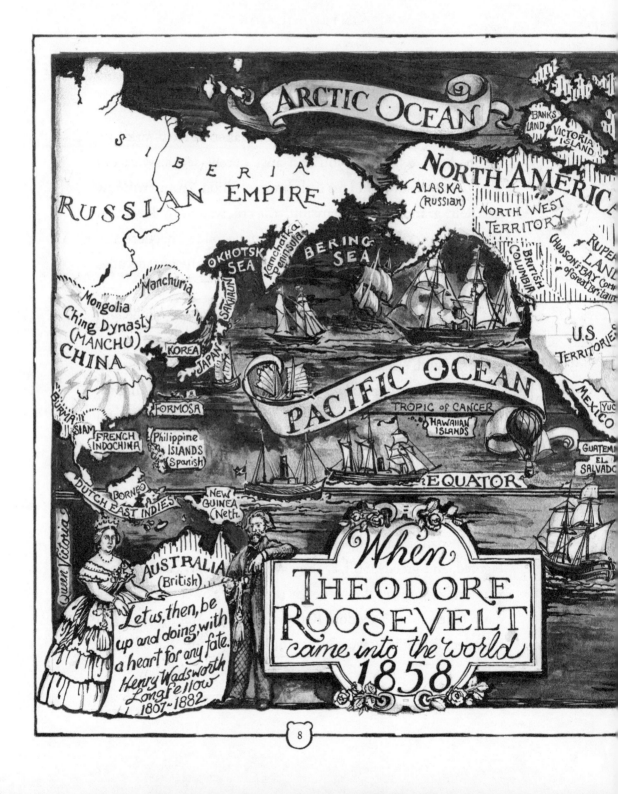

Sunday afternoon in Teedie's New York

CHAPTER ONE

The Roosevelts of 20th Street

TEEDIE'S WORLD

MOST FOLKS MAKING THEIR WAY HOME or out for a stroll on the night of October 27, 1858, had no particular reason to notice the building at 28 East 20th Street. If they knew that a child was being born there, passersby might smile at an upstairs window or give their shoulders a shrug as they walked on down the street. After all, babies were born every day. On that autumn night in New York City, not even the baby's parents knew that a particularly remarkable life had begun. But it had: Theodore Roosevelt was born.

1858   Note: The time line features events that took place around the world during TR's lifetime.

Henry Wadsworth Longfellow *publishes his bestseller, The Courtship of Miles Standish.*

May 11 –
Minnesota is the 32nd state.

Sept. 16 – Oct. 10 – The first run of the Butterfield Overland Mail takes place. Stagecoaches carry letters from St. Louis to San Francisco in 23 days, 23 hours.

Dec. 22 –
Giacomo Puccini, *composer of swell operas, is born in Italy.*

The Roosevelts' **NEW YORK CITY 1858**

½ mile 1

Frederick Law OLMSTED and Calvert VAUX are designing CENTRAL PARK

42nd ST.

Broadway (Bloomingdale Road)

Long Acre Square (now known as TIMES SQUARE)

CROTON Reservoir, on land now occupied by the NEW YORK public library

34th ST.

9th AVE.
8th AVE.
7th AVE.

5th Ave.

HUDSON RIVER - RAILROAD

MADISON SQUARE

TR's house 28 East 20th St.

R.H. MACY's

UNION SQUARE

A.T. STEWART's Marble Palace

WASHINGTON SQUARE

GRAMERCY PARK

20th ST.

QUEENS

Newtown creek

NEW JERSEY

Hudson River

CANAL ST.

BROADWAY

BOWERY

14th ST.

THOMPKINS SQUARE

East River

LONG ISLAND

In 1898, BROOKLYN and communities in QUEENS, the BRONX, and on STATEN ISLAND will join with MANHATTAN to form GREATER NEW YORK

Washington MARKET PARK

Park Theater

HARRY HALL's Dance Hall

HOUSTON ST.

P.T. BARNUM'S American Museum

CITY HALL

FIVE POINTS

LOWER EAST SIDE

Trinity Church

St. Paul's CHAPEL

WATER ST.

Castle Garden

Custom HOUSE

WALL ST.

the Battery

BROOKLYN HEIGHTS

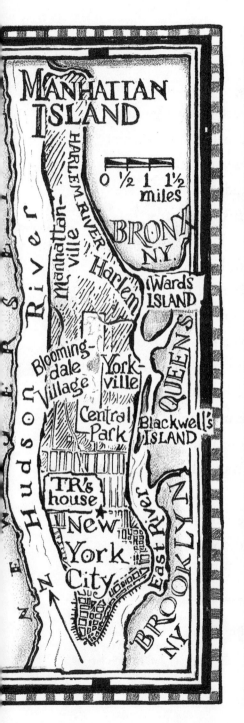

NEW YORK CITY
1858

At the southernmost tip of Manhattan Island, more and more immigrants are arriving at Castle Garden. (Ellis Island won't open for business until 1892.) These folks, mostly from Germany and the British Isles, will do their best to climb New York City's social staircase, but life on its bottom steps is hard. In neighborhoods like the Five Points, kids who live past babyhood – more than half won't – might try to survive by joining a gang like the Bowery Boys, the Plug Uglies, or the Dead Rabbits. New York's streets are a smelly, noisy chaos of wagons, carts, omnibuses, and buggies, pulled by thousands of horses. Folks are going to P. T. Barnum's American Museum to see for themselves the Feejee Mermaid or the world-famous midget General Tom Thumb. They shop at R. H. Macy's brand-new store or at the country's first department store, A. T. Stewart's immense Marble Palace. Up north of the city, work is beginning on Central Park. Pigs and goats wander about farms scattered among villages, such as Harlem, Bloomingdale, and Yorkville.

What was happening in baby Theodore's world? Plenty!

Men were struggling to string wire cable along the floor of the Atlantic so people could telegraph messages from one side of the ocean to the other. Far away in Egypt, workers were getting ready to start digging the long-awaited Suez Canal so ships will be able to sail the Mediterranean to the Red Sea and the Indian Ocean. People in India were struggling, as deadly uprisings were breaking out between native Indians and British overlords.

The British Empire was growing so rich in industries and colonies that this whole time in history will be known as the Victorian Age, named after Britain's Queen Victoria. In 1858, she was a third of the way through her 63-year reign. One of her subjects, Charles Darwin, was working on a book about evolution, a theory that he's been working on. It will fire up a generation's curiosity about the natural world and inspire hot discussions to this very day. Charles Dickens was writing his masterpiece, *A Tale of Two Cities*. Two other Englishmen, Richard Burton and John Hanning Speke, were exploring the land roundabout Africa's Lake Tanganyika.

Czar Alexander II was trying to better the lives of poor Russians. Suffering, death, and civil war were ripping across vast

1859

Feb. 14 —
Oregon is the 33rd state.

April 4 —
A New York City audience hears the first performance of **Dan Emmett**'s new song "Dixie."

June 30 —
Charles Blondin becomes the first daredevil to cross Niagara Falls on a tightrope.

Oct. 16 — Harpers Ferry, VA —
Men led by abolitionist **John Brown** raid the U.S. arsenal, stealing guns they hope to use in their effort to free the southern slaves. It won't work out that way (see Dec. 2).

China. Meanwhile, the U.S. President, James Buchanan, was trying to calm his own countrymen, who were getting more and more divided and worked up over the nasty fact that in America's South millions of black folks were enslaved.

HOUSE DIVIDED

IN CONGRESS, IN BARNS, SALOONS, AND KITCHENS, folks discussed the slavery question. The argument had gone on since the nation's beginning, but *abolitionists* (folks who wanted slavery stopped) were gaining strength, spurred on by passionate speakers, such as Frederick Douglass and Sojourner Truth, and by America's expansion. Would slavery spread into new western territories? Already pro- and anti-slavery people were killing each other out in Missouri and Kansas. In 1858, thousands came to listen as two politicians, tall, clean-shaven Abraham Lincoln

1859   **1860**

Dec. 2 —
John Brown *is hanged in Charles Town, Virginia.*

April 3 – 13 —
The U.S. Mail is carried on the first relay run of the Pony Express, from St. Joseph, MO, to Sacramento, CA.

Giuseppe Garibaldi *and his thousand-man force of "red shirts" fight for a united Italy.*

and Illinois's powerful Senator Stephen Douglas, argued over America's dilemma. Thousands more read about the famous Lincoln-Douglas debates in the nation's newspapers. In 1859, bullets flew, people died, and fiery abolitionist John Brown got himself hanged when he tried to start a slave uprising.

As for the Roosevelts, Theodore, Sr. (our Theodore's dad and known in the family as Thee) had grown up in New York, where owning slaves had been against the law since 1828. On the other hand, his wife Martha (a.k.a. Mittie) came from Georgia, where slavery was a fact of everyday life. When Thee Roosevelt married beautiful Mittie Bulloch in 1853, her mom sold four slaves to pay for the wedding. In the late 1850s and early 1860s, the Roosevelts' happy family was overshadowed by the nation's troubles. Both were growing right along.

Thee and Mittie doted on their daughter, Anna, who was born in 1855. They called her Bamie (pronounced "bammie," from the word "bambina"). Then, in 1858, came baby Theodore (Teedie) and Elliott (Ellie) in 1860. The next year, Corinne (Conie) completed the nicknaming Roosevelts, a close family who did their best not to let bad health dampen high spirits. Sad to say, but the Roosevelt kids had loads of ailments.

1860

Nov. 6 —
Republican
Abraham Lincoln
is elected 16th
U.S. President.

Dec. 20 —
The states are no longer united, as South Carolina becomes the first state to secede from (leave) the United States. Claiming a constitutional right to own and regulate their slaves, ten more states break away. The rebellious eleven call themselves the Confederate States of America.

Mittie and her four little Roosevelts

Because of a painful sort of tuberculosis in the bones of her back, tiny, sober-faced Bamie had to wear a heavy steel brace. When she was four, a new doctor helped her to move more freely, but she'd never be entirely comfortable, and her spine would never be straight. Elliott would be plagued with headaches, occasional seizures, and – as a man – alcoholism. Asthma attacked Corinne from time to time, but it was far worse for delicate Teedie.

1860	1861		
Frederick Walton *invents* linoleum, *a kind of floor covering.*	**Czar Alexander II** *frees 20 million serfs (Russian peasants) from having to farm land owned by aristocrats.*	**Charles Dickens** *writes* Great Expectations. *The skeleton of an archaeopteryx, the earliest bird, is found in Germany.*	 *Jan. 29 — Kansas is the 34th state.*

He was three when asthma began clamping his airways shut: very scary! "One of my memories," Theodore wrote, "is of my father walking up and down the room with me in his arms at night when I was a very small person, and of sitting up in bed gasping, with my father and mother trying to help me." Unfortunately, no one then quite knew how. Some doctors thought that nicotine or caffeine would help break the disease's grip, so more than a few desperate parents, including Mittie and Thee, gave their gasping little kids cigars to puff or coffee to sip.

A breathless night in the nursery

1861

Mar. 17 —
A united
Kingdom of
Italy is
proclaimed.

July 21 —
Manassas, VA —
First Battle of
Bull Run
is fought (3,500
casualties: dead,
wounded, missing).

Oct. 24 —
The first transcontinental
telegraph message travels
far and away faster
than horses can run.
The days of the Pony
Express are over.

Far better, as far as Teedie was concerned, was when his dad would bundle him up and take him out in the carriage. Off the horses would fly through the dark streets of the city, hoofbeats echoing. In the rushing night air, in his father's arms, Teedie could breathe.

Teedie delighted in his beautiful mom. Mittie's skin was moonlight pale, her hair glossy black. She told wonderful stories, too, but it was Thee who made the biggest impression on the little boy.

"I never knew anyone who got greater joy out of living," Theodore later wrote, "than did my father." Tall, powerful Thee had piercing blue eyes and a golden brown beard. He loved his family, fine clothes, and fast horses. In describing him, people used the word *leonine* (like a lion). Every week, rich, handsome Thee taught Sunday school. Every day, his children waited for him to come downstairs, each hoping to be the lucky one who sat closest to him as he conducted morning prayers. Thee had firm notions on how good people should act: Work hard. Be helpful and brave. And they must never sink their teeth into their siblings, as four-year-old Teedie discovered when he bit Bamie's arm. It was the only time his dad ever spanked him.

1861   1862

Dec. 14 — **Prince Albert,** **Queen** **Victoria's** husband, dies in London.	**Victor Hugo** *writes Les Miserables.* Faster way to shoot. **R.J. Gatling** *designs the first practical machine gun.*	COCHISE	Apache leader **Cochise** *leads hundreds of warriors against thousands of settlers in present- day Arizona and New Mexico.*	Feb. 5 — **Julia Ward** **Howe's** *poem "The Battle Hymn of the Republic" is published.*

It wasn't enough for Thee to bring Bamie ice cream when she was suffering. He helped start the New York Orthopedic Hospital. He didn't just slip a nickel into the hand of one of the city's many homeless kids. He found them foster homes and helped begin the Newsboys' Lodging House and the Children's Aid Society. Because Thee had high hopes for his big, rough city, he helped launch the American Museum of Natural History. In 1869, the papers were signed in his front parlor. A year later, he'd be in on the beginning of the Metropolitan Museum of Art.

In 1861, the Civil War broke out. How four-year-old Teedie would have loved for his big, tall dad to put on a blue Yankee uniform – with a sword! To Teedie, war was a glorious adventure, a time for men to be heroes. At bedtime, he prayed to the Lord to "grind the Southern troops to powder!" His mom's sister, Aunt Anna, who'd come, along with Grandmamma Bulloch, to live with Mittie, hid a smile and the fact that the three women were smuggling secret packages of clothes, medicine, and money (behind Thee's back) to their dear ones down South. Mittie begged her husband not to go to war. But President Lincoln was calling for men to fight to save the nation.

What was honorable, pro-Union Thee to do?

1862

Feb. 10 –
Washington, DC –
Typhoid fever kills
Willie Lincoln,
11-year-old son of
the President.

Feb. 22 –
Jefferson Davis
becomes president of
the C.S.A. (Confederate
States of America).

Mar. 9 –
Confederate frigate Virginia,
a.k.a. Merrimack, retreats
after tangling with Union
Monitor. This clash of the
ironclads means the end of
wooden warships.

Teedie prays for Union victory

Like many well-to-do men, he paid for a man to fight in his place, but he still served his country. Thee visited the President and the soldiers' camps. He worked hard, making sure that the troops were clothed and fed, setting things up so that they could send part of their paychecks home to their suffering families, and helping wounded, crippled veterans find jobs. It was noble, necessary work, but to Teedie – well! It was pretty watery stuff compared to his dashing Bulloch uncles in the Confederate Navy. He wanted his dad to be equally heroic for the Union.

1862

April 6 – 7 –
Pittsburg Landing, TN –
Battle of Shiloh is fought
(23,500 casualties).

May 20 –
Congress passes the Homestead
Act. The U.S. will give 160
acres of public land to any
citizen over 21 who works the
land for 5 years or pays $1.25
per acre for it.

June 10 –
Dorothea L. Dix
becomes superintendent
of the female nurses
who will be tending
sick and wounded
Union soldiers.

The CIVIL WAR 1861~1865

SALINEVILLE
JULY 26, '63

OHIO
MORGAN, 1863

LEXINGTON
X Sept. 18-21, '61

WESTPORT
Oct. 23, 64

ST. LOUIS

INDIANA

WEST VIRGINIA

MISSOURI

ILLINOIS

OHIO RIVER

KENTUCKY

WILSON'S CREEK
Aug. 10, '61

MISSISSIPPI RIVER

PRICE, 1864

FORT DONELSON
Feb 12-16, '62

PERRYVILLE
Oct. 8, '62

More than 2,100 battles are fought in VIRGINIA
(April 17, '61)

PEA RIDGE
(Elkhorn Tavern)
Mar. 7-8, '62

NASHVILLE
Dec. 15-16, '64

TENNESSEE
(June 8, '61)

ARKANSAS
(May 6, '61)

MEMPHIS
June 6, '62

SHILOH
(Pittsburg Landing)
April 6-7, '62

FRANKLIN
Nov. 30, '64

CHATTANOOGA
Nov. 23-25, '63

CHICKAMAUGA
Sept. 19-20, '63

GRANT

MISSISSIPPI
(Jan. 9, '61)

HOOD
1864

ATLANTA
captured
Sept 2, '64

SABINE
X CROSS ROADS
April 8, '64

VICKSBURG
July 4, '63

JACKSON
captured
May 14, '63

ALABAMA
(Jan 11, '61)

MONTGOMERY
CSA capital
Feb~May, '61

WILSON
1865

SHERMAN
1864

SHERMAN 1865

SAVANNAH
occupied
Dec. 21, '64

TEXAS
(Feb. 1, '61)

LOUISIANA
(Jan. 26, '61)

MOBILE BAY
blockaded
Aug. 5, '64

GEORGIA
(Jan. 19, '61)

JACKSONVILLE
occupied
Feb. 7, '64

The last battle of the CIVIL WAR was fought at PALMITO RANCH, TEXAS, near the mouth of the RIO GRANDE. May 13, 1865 ~ a CONFEDERATE victory.

NEW ORLEANS
occupied
April 25, '62

FLORIDA
(Jan. 10, '61)

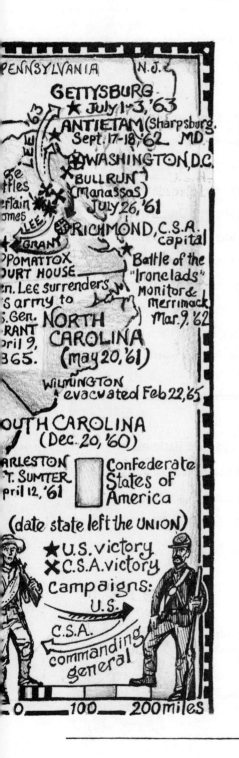

THE WAR BETWEEN THE STATES

It proved to be every bit as difficult for Abraham Lincoln and his generation to reunite the republic as it had been for George Washington and his fellow Americans to form the nation in the first place. How could people be enslaved in a free country? And how much could a central government boss the states and the citizens? The long argument over these questions led to four horrid years of sacrifice, torn-apart families, and more than 10,000 battles. The Civil War cost $15 billion in money and property; not until well into the 20th century would the ruined South recover.

Even worse, the war took the lives of about 600,000 soldiers, robbing the world of all that they might have achieved. Men fought with almost unimaginable courage for the Union, for their homeland, for one another, against one another, and for freedom. Countless Americans, including four million freed slaves, had their lives forever changed. As for keeping the nation united and strong, that's our job.

ORPHAN TRAINS

Thousands of homeless children prowled New York City. "Street Arabs" they were called, as if the mean streets were a desert with scarcely an oasis where they might find food and shelter. In 1853, Charles Loring Brace, Theodore Roosevelt, Sr., and some of their friends came up with a plan to save the kids. They began the Children's Aid Society. They felt that it was their duty "to get these children of unhappy fortune utterly out of their surroundings," Brace wrote, "and to send them away to kind Christian homes in the country." For nearly 75 years, the society gathered up orphaned or abandoned kids. Sometimes, neglectful parents allowed their children to be taken away — to a better life, they hoped. Each child was given a little Bible and a change of clothes and put aboard a westbound

Almost to the end of his life, there'd always be a little bit of Teedie in Theodore Roosevelt, along with his memories of what his father did – and did not do – when war trumpets sounded.

Less than three weeks after Confederate General Lee surrendered his army to Union General Grant on April 9, 1865,

1862

Aug. 17 —
Starving Lakota people (a.k.a. Sioux) rise up against white settlers in Minnesota. In December, at Mankato, 38 leaders of the uprising will be hanged.

Sept. 17 —
Sharpsburg, MD — Battle at Antietam Creek is fought (26,250 casualties).

Sept. 22 —
President Lincoln *issues the Emancipation Proclamation. As of Jan. 1, 1863, slaves in rebellious states shall be free.*

"orphan train." When one chugged into town, would-be parents or anyone in need of an extra kitchen worker, babysitter, or field hand went to the courthouse or the town hall to take their pick of the tired, confused children put there on display. If the child agreed, the deal was done on the spot. Over the years, way too few Aid Society people checked on the kids. Some of the homes were far from kind. Some children ran away, but for the most part, old and young made the best of things. In time, more than 100,000 children, including this author's Great Aunt Alice, rode the orphan trains.

Teedie and his little brother were at one of the tall windows in their grandfather Cornelius Roosevelt's mansion. From there they saw President Lincoln's funeral parade pass by. For a little while, Corinne's playmate, three-year-old Edith Carow, watched too. But she began to cry, so the boys shut her in a closet.

1862   1863

Dec. 13 —
Battle of
Fredericksburg
(17,500 casualties) is
fought in Virginia.

Feb. 2 —
Samuel Clemens
trots out a new pen
name: **Mark Twain.**

Feb. 10 — *New York City —*
Showman **P. T. Barnum** *stages*
a big wedding for his big star,
Charles S. Stratton, *2'5" tall,*
a.k.a. **General Tom Thumb,**
and his diminutive bride, 2'8"
Mercy Lavinia Warren.

ROMANCE AND ADVENTURE

ILLNESSES KEPT YOUNG THEODORE RELATIVELY ISOLATED from other kids. Except for a brief stab at private school, he was mostly home-schooled by tutors, by Aunt Anna in particular. He read, squinting, piles and piles of books. (Not until he was almost 14 would he realize how nearsighted he was and get his first pair of glasses.) He adored reading adventure stories about heroic struggles against the forces of nature. Who'd have guessed that Teedie, the pale, timid, city boy, would come face to face with the amazing, challenging natural world as he walked up Broadway to buy strawberries?

There it was, on a slab at the fish market. The minute he saw it, Theodore the Naturalist was born. He stared into its blank eyes. He asked about it. He came back again and again to measure it and ponder the rotting remnants of the dead seal, an amazing

1863

May 19 – July 4 —
Union forces capture Vicksburg, Mississippi (29,000 casualties).

June 20 —
West Virginia breaks away from Confederate Virginia and becomes the 35th state in the Union.

July 1–3 —
Terrible bloodshed and a Union victory result from the Battle of Gettysburg, in Pennsylvania.

July —
News that men will be drafted for the war sparks awful riots in New York City.

creature that used to swim in the vast, cold, sublime depths of the salty sea. Theodore never forgot how the sight of that seal filled him "with every possible feeling of romance and adventure." He didn't mean "romance" in a smoochy way. No, he meant the stuff of high ideals, heroic and noble clashes between man and wild nature. Eventually, the market man gave the spindly little kid with all the questions the seal's skull to have for his very own.

Teedie and the seal

That seal sparked Teedie's passion for observing, collecting, dissecting, studying, drawing, hunting, shooting, skinning, stuffing, labeling, and writing about the creatures of the natural world. By the time he was nine years old, Teedie had collected all manner of bugs, feathers, and such – and four live mice. When they weren't trying to crawl down the young naturalist's neck, they lived in cages alongside the seal skull and the rest of the

1863

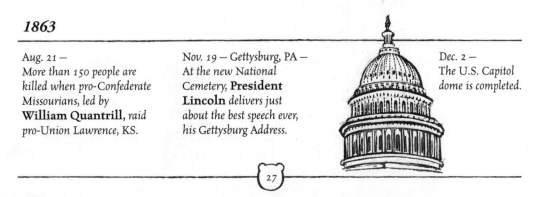

Aug. 21 —
More than 150 people are killed when pro-Confederate Missourians, led by **William Quantrill,** *raid pro-Union Lawrence, KS.*

Nov. 19 – Gettysburg, PA —
At the new National Cemetery, **President Lincoln** *delivers just about the best speech ever, his Gettysburg Address.*

Dec. 2 —
The U.S. Capitol dome is completed.

"Roosevelt Museum of Natural History." It was housed in an upstairs bookcase far from disapproving chambermaids, who never forgot the dead mouse they found in the icebox. It was hard to say who'd been more outraged, the cook who pitched the corpse into the dust bin or Teedie. He'd been preserving it for a scientific experiment.

The Roosevelts set off to sea.

In the spring of 1869, all the servants at 28 East 20th Street were rushing about, packing valises and trunks for the Roosevelt family vacation. Mittie wanted to see her brothers, who, like many disappointed ex-Confederates, had gone to live in England.

1864

Jan. 13 —
Composer **Stephen C. Foster** *dies, having written* "Beautiful Dreamer," *his last song.*

Mar. 9 —
Ulysses S. Grant *becomes the Union's General-in-Chief.*

Nov. 8. —
The U.S. conducts a national election in the middle of a civil war: Pretty amazing! **Abraham Lincoln** *is reelected.*

She and Thee wanted their children to see Europe, and they hoped that sea air and foreign climates would help Teedie breathe.

You'd have thought that ten-year-old Teedie would have gotten a large bang out of such an adventure, but no. Seasickness, asthma, aunts who kissed too much, museums, and cathedrals were tough. Still, he wasn't sick all the time. He peppered his diary with accounts of good days. The Roosevelt kids played in the hotels, pillow-fighting and tormenting the staff. Thee took them hiking in the Swiss Alps and climbing on Vesuvius, Italy's ancient volcano. Upon seeing "a red flame inside the mountain," Teedie plunged his walking stick into the hole. "It caught fire right away."

Rocky on the outside, fiery on the inside!

1864

Nov. 16 – Dec. 20 — U.S. **General William T. Sherman**'s *Yankee soldiers trample central Georgia on their "March to the Sea," from Atlanta to Savannah.*

Louis Pasteur *invents pasteurization, a process to sterilize milk.*

Science fiction writer **Jules Verne** *publishes* A Journey to the Center of the Earth.

His parents couldn't help noticing that all of the physical activity was good for Teedie. Back home again in New York, lion-like Thee had a talk with his spindly cub.

"Theodore, you have the mind but you have not the body, and without the body the mind cannot go as far as it should."

Getting stronger every day

Father and son gazed at each other, their blue eyes blazing. "You must make your body."

It would be hard work, Thee knew, but he said firmly, "I know you will do it."

Teedie promised his father, and he promised himself: He would be his body's master and make it as powerful as his mind and his will.

The turning point is a noble notion – the idea that up until a certain instant, you'd gone one way, and all was this,

1865

April 14 –
Washington, DC –
Actor **John Wilkes Booth** *shoots*
President Abraham Lincoln, *who dies the following morning.*

April 15 –
Vice President
Andrew Johnson
becomes the 17th U.S. President.

April 26 –
Bowling Green, VA –
Assassin **John Wilkes Booth** *is captured and killed.*

then you'd decide to go another way, and from that time on all would be that. It was that sort of lightning-bolt moment for young Theodore.

He used up every scrap of spare time lifting weights, doing all sorts of exercises, practicing gymnastics in the gym his father had fixed for him, and taking wrestling lessons. When a couple of bigger kids teased and shoved him around a bit, he took up the manly art of boxing. When he and his family left the city for the country (out on Long Island, generally), Teedie rode his horse and climbed hills and trees. He hiked, swam, and worked the oars on his rowboat. Murdering hot, numbing cold, or raining cats and dogs, Theodore refused to be discouraged. He discovered that he liked the feel of pushing himself to the limit and beyond. The harder the effort, the more fun he had.

For the rest of his life, stubborn, passionate Theodore kept the promises he made to his father and to himself when he was a timid, skinny boy at the crossroads.

1865

April 27 —
Death on the Mississippi! Nearly 1,500 people die when the boilers blow on the steamboat Sultana. *Many are Union soldiers heading home.*

May 10 —
*Irwinville, GA —
C.S.A. President* **Jefferson Davis** *is captured.*

May 26 —
The American Civil War is officially over.

Young Theodore in the great outdoors

CHAPTER TWO

Coming of Age

EGYPT

IN 1872, AS PRESIDENT ULYSSES S. GRANT was getting reelected, the Roosevelt family went abroad again, this time to Egypt, arriving at Alexandria at the end of November.

"Egypt," 14-year-old Teedie exulted in his diary, "the most ancient of countries! A land that was old when Rome was bright, was old when Babylon was in its glory."

Like many Victorian travelers, the Roosevelts hired Egyptians to take them and their rented *dahabeah* (houseboat) down the Nile. With his new glasses, Teedie could appreciate

1865

Pulaski, TN —
Confederate veterans form a club, the Ku Klux Klan (KKK). Soon its white-robed and hooded members are terrorizing and killing their black neighbors and anyone who is on their side. The KKK will be outlawed in 1871 (see 1915).

Dec. 6 —
The 13th Amendment makes slavery illegal in the U.S. The long, rocky road to patch things up with the ruined states of the defeated Confederacy is called Reconstruction (see 1877).

ancient tombs and temples. With his new shotgun, he blasted away at beasts living in the river reeds and at herons, owls, and larks. It was his "first real collecting as a student of natural history." Poring over his books, using the artistic and scientific skills he'd learned in his taxidermy lessons plus a certain amount of arsenic and formaldehyde, grubby, smelly, happy Teedie skinned, stuffed, studied, and classified his specimens. This is what a naturalist did back in the day. "I have procured

Taxidermy on the River Nile

1865

Lewis Carroll (*a.k.a.* **C. L. Dodgson**) *writes* Alice's Adventures in Wonderland.

1866

For the first time, cowboys drive cattle down the Chisholm Trail to Abilene, KS.

Botanist, monk, and pioneer in the science of genetics, **Gregor Mendel** *publishes his studies on heredity.*

Leo Tolstoy *begins publishing* War and Peace.

between one and two hundred skins," Theodore wrote proudly.

On they traveled through Palestine and into Europe. There Teedie, Elliott, and Corinne would be staying with a professor's family in Dresden, Germany, learning the language, studying math and other subjects. In between lessons, asthma attacks, and a case of the mumps, Teedie sandwiched scientific expeditions. "Whenever I could get out into the country," he wrote, "I collected specimens industriously and enlivened the household with hedgehogs and other small beasts and reptiles which persisted in escaping from partially closed drawers."

When the family returned to New York City, it was to a big new house at 6 West 57th Street. No longer was Theodore the odd little boy, known to stash frogs in his hat or snakes in the water pitcher. Asthma still attacked him, but less and less often. He'd grown into a curious combination of body-builder, outdoor guy, constant reader, and budding writer, though he'd always be a lousy speller. In fact, one day, as President, he'd launch a campaign to make words simpler to spell. For now though, in 1873, with his rapid-fire way of talking, his glasses (relatively rare back then), and the fact that he often smelled of chemicals, bird guts, and grubby teenager, Theodore was a bit of an odd duck. All of

1867

Austria and Hungary unite under **Emperor Franz Josef I.**

Swedish chemist **Alfred Nobel** invents dynamite.

Johann Strauss, Jr. composes "The Blue Danube," his totally famous waltz.

Feb. 7 —
Laura Ingalls Wilder, future author of the Little House books, is born in Wisconsin.

Mar. 1 – **Nebraska** is the 37th state.

his reading, tutoring, and travels taught him how to speak and understand French and German. He knew geography, history, and, of course, loads of natural science. But if he was going to pass the tests to get into college, he would need some extra help, so his dad hired a tutor.

Work hard, play hard, that was Theodore's way. Being strangled by the mysterious asthma taught him that death hovered behind the next breath. Life was precious and not to be wasted. When he and his family went to their summerhouse at Oyster Bay, Theodore made time to study all right. And he walked and rode through the woods and rowed and swam in Long Island Sound with Corinne, Elliott, and their friend Edith. He passed

Row, row, rowing with Edith and Corinne

1867

Mar. 30 —
The Congress agrees to a deal set up by Secretary of State **William H. Seward**. *The U.S. will pay Russia $7,200,000 for Alaska territory, a.k.a. "Seward's Folly."*

1868

Nov. 7—
Marie Sklodowska Curie, *future physicist, is born in Poland (see 1903).*

Louisa May Alcott *writes* Little Women.

Engineer **Robert Whitehead** *develops the first practical underwater torpedo.*

the entrance exams. At the end of the summer of 1876, 17-year-old Theodore would be off to college at Harvard.

THE U.S. AT 100

THAT SUMMER OF 1876 WAS A BIG DEAL for the nation, too. A century had passed since the colonial delegates agreed to sign the Declaration of Independence. Americans marked the occasion with a world's fair, Philadelphia's Centennial Exposition. President Ulysses S. Grant and millions of others came to taste their first root beer; pay 10 cents for a weird tropical fruit, the newly imported banana; and marvel at the latest technologies, such as Alexander Graham Bell's astonishing new electrical device that could send a person's voice along wires to someone else's ear. People buzzed about Mark Twain's latest book, *The Adventures of Tom Sawyer*. And there was a shocking story in the

1868

Emperor Mutsuhito

Jan. 3 — Japan —
The era of the shoguns (military leaders) ends. **Emperor Mutsuhito** *holds traditional power. Japan's capital moves from Kyoto to Edo, renamed Tokyo.*

May 26 —
Radical Republicans want to force **President Andrew Johnson** *out of office, but he survives his impeachment trial in the U.S. Senate.*

Nov. 3—
War hero **Ulysses S. Grant** *is elected 18th U.S. President.*

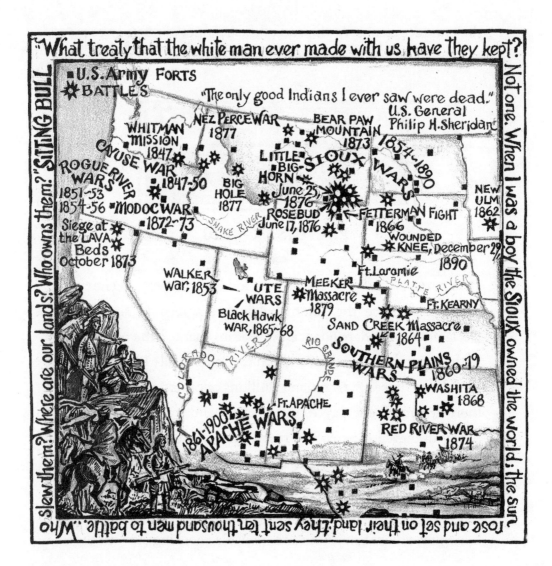

"What treaty that the white man ever made with us have they kept?"

"SITTING BULL"

Not one. When I was a boy the Sioux owned the world; the sun rose and set on their land; they sent ten thousand men to battle.. Who slew them? Where are our lands? Who owns them?

■ U.S. Army FORTS
✴ BATTLES

"The only good Indians I ever saw were dead."
U.S. General Philip H. Sheridan

WHITMAN MISSION 1847
CAYUSE WAR 1847-50
NEZ PERCE WAR 1877
BEAR PAW MOUNTAIN 1873
SIOUX WARS 1854~1890
ROGUE RIVER WARS 1851-53 1854-56
LITTLE BIG HORN June 25, 1876
MODOC WAR 1872-73
BIG HOLE 1877
ROSEBUD June 17, 1876
SNAKE RIVER
FETTERMAN FIGHT 1866
NEW ULM 1862
Siege at the LAVA Beds October 1873
WOUNDED KNEE, December 29, 1890
Ft. Laramie
PLATTE RIVER
WALKER War, 1853
UTE WARS
MEEKER Massacre 1879
Ft. KEARNY
Black Hawk WAR, 1865~68
SAND CREEK Massacre 1864
COLORADO RIVER
RIO GRANDE
SOUTHERN PLAINS WARS 1860-79
WASHITA 1868
Ft. APACHE
1861-1900 APACHE WARS
RED RIVER WAR 1874

1869

Yokohama, Japan —
Jonathan Scobie
*invents the jinrikisha
(rickshaw).*

*Egypt —
The Suez Canal
is completed.*

*Ohio — The Cincinnati
Red Stockings become
the first professional
baseball team.*

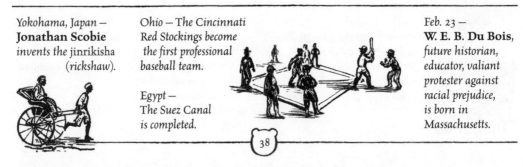

Feb. 23 —
W. E. B. Du Bois,
*future historian,
educator, valiant
protester against
racial prejudice,
is born in
Massachusetts.*

newspapers about General Custer's fatal clash with Crazy Horse and legions of Lakota and Cheyenne warriors out in Montana Territory at the Battle of Little Bighorn.

The 100-year-old nation numbered 38 states and, with the 1876 election, it would have its 19th consecutive President, but not until 1877 could anyone say for certain who that would be. More votes were cast for Democrat Samuel J. Tilden, but Rutherford B. Hayes, the Republican, won in the Electoral College. True to the behind-the-scenes deal (with powerful Southern politicians) that won him the election, President Hayes would end Reconstruction and pull federal troops out of the Southern states, where they'd been patrolling since the end of the Civil War. Millions of former slaves and their families would be left to the mercies of their white neighbors. Look out.

And what was the state of Theodore Roosevelt in 1876? According to his own scientific measurements, he stood 5'8" and weighed 124 pounds. His hair was fair and wavy; fashionable whiskers grew on the sides of his firm-featured face. Still fresh in his mind was the advice he'd received when his dad took college-bound Theodore to the train: "Take care of your morals first," said Thee, "your health next and finally your studies."

1869

May 10 —
Promontory Point, Utah —
Tracks of the Union Pacific
Railroad and those of the
Central Pacific are joined with
a golden spike and a big fat
celebration. America's trans-
continental railroad is complete.

Oct. 2 —
**Mohandes
"Mahatma"
Gandhi**, future
peacemaker and
statesman, is born
in India.

Nov. 6 —
First college football
game is played.
Rutgers beats the
College of New
Jersey (now known
as Princeton) 6–4.

A BRAVE CHRISTIAN GENTLEMAN

THEODORE SETTLED HIMSELF INTO A SECOND-FLOOR ROOM in a house in Cambridge, Massachusetts. Stuffed birds under glass domes perched on the bookcases and antlers festooned the walls. Snakes and turtles lived in a cage. He was one of 821 students – all men – at Harvard that year, and not one of them was like Theodore. Most walked between classes. He trotted. Plenty of them seemed bored with their classes. Not Theodore. He studied hard, talked fast, and asked so many questions that one professor finally burst out, "Now look here, Roosevelt, let me talk!"

Theodore worked out every afternoon and, like his dad, taught Sunday school on the weekends. He went to football games and parties, but when it came to drinking, smoking, and dating, he thanked Heaven in his diary that he was "perfectly pure." Lots of fellows were cool. Theodore burned

1869

1870

Dec. 9 – Philadelphia, PA – The Knights of Labor, one of the first big unions, is founded.

Archaeologist **Heinrich Schliemann** begins digging, searching for the ancient city of Troy.

Lots and lots of diamonds are discovered in the southern tip of Africa, deepening the rivalry between British colonists and the Boers (Dutch settlers).

hot. He had a noble father he was trying to live up to.

"I am sure that there is no one who has a Father who is also his best and most intimate friend, as you are mine," Theodore wrote to him. "I shall do my best to earn your trust."

Theodore at Harvard

It would be hard for almost anyone to hear that their father was sick. For Theodore, in his second year of college, and for his sisters and brother, it was downright dreadful. Lion-like Theodore, Sr., was the mainstay of all their lives. "Greatheart," some called him, for all that he'd done for others. Now, in the fall and winter of 1877–78, stomach cancer was killing him.

As Theodore made his way home, worrying and praying, Thee was suffering in Elliott's arms. Theodore Roosevelt, Sr., only 46 years old, died late in the cold, rainy night of February 9, 1878.

1870

Feb. 3 —
The 15th Amendment becomes law. Now the vote cannot be denied because a citizen is black.

Feb. 25—
Hiram R. Revels of Mississippi becomes the first African-American U.S. Senator.

July 19 —
Napoleon III *of France declares war on Prussia. For the French people, the months to come will be a terrible time of hunger and unrest, violent and deadly.*

Oct. 12 –
Ex-C.S.A. **General Robert E. Lee**, 63, dies in Lexington, VA.

Flags in New York City were already being lowered for Thee when his older son arrived.

As passionately as he did everything else, 19-year-old Theodore grieved for his father, "the best man I ever knew." He poured out his energy, galloping his horse, rowing his boat for miles and miles. He poured his feelings into his diary. To be worthy of the memory of his forever-idealized dad, Theodore vowed "to study well and live like a brave Christian gentleman."

SUNSHINE

WHAT ON EARTH COULD POSSIBLY BEGIN TO MEND the huge hole torn in Theodore's life? He kept busy. For one thing, he did indeed "study well" and made Phi Beta Kappa. You have to make very good grades for that honor. For another, he packed his social life with friends and clubs – the Natural History Society, for

1871

New York reporters investigate, **Thomas Nast** draws fierce political cartoons, and lawyer **Samuel Tilden** (see 1876) leads the attack that nails corrupt politician **William M. "Boss" Tweed**. As head of Tammany Hall (the Democratic political machine), he'd swiped millions of dollars of public money for himself and his cronies.

Changes in Japan cause samurai warriors to lose their power and privileges.

instance, Hasty Pudding, and the very choosy Porcellian Club. Tone-deaf Theodore even signed up for the glee club! He helped to edit a college magazine and began work on the first of the 36 books he'd write, a history of the sea battles in the War of 1812. He went hunting in Maine, then, back at school, he squeezed parties, ice skating, carriage- and sleigh-riding, and dances into his days and nights. One of his partners remembered that bouncy Theodore didn't so much dance as, well, "he hopped!" Oh, and another thing: He fell in love.

As often happens, how hard you fall has a lot to do with how bad you were feeling before you met the adored object. Not quite nine months after his father's death, Theodore met one of his classmate's cousins, Alice Lee, known as "Sunshine" to her family. Hopping and whirling around polished dance floors with beautiful, cheerful Alice went a long way toward mending Theodore's heart. He forgot whatever romance he'd had with his childhood friend, freckled, auburn-haired Edith Carow. Theodore went completely nuts about Alice, courted her, and convinced her to be his bride. Theodore graduated in June. Then, on his 22nd birthday, October 27, 1880, Alice Hathaway Lee married the man she called Teddy or, sometimes, *Teddykins*.

1871

Jan. 18 —
*Like Italy, Germany had been a crazy quilt of kingdoms, duchies, and principalities. Now it unites under the rule of **Emperor Wilhelm I** and his prime minister **Count von Bismarck**, the "Iron Chancellor."*

April 10 — Brooklyn, NY —
***P. T. Barnum** opens the Great Traveling Museum, Menagerie, Caravan, and Hippodrome. Next year, his Greatest Show on Earth will be the first circus to travel by train.*

You might like to know that Bamie's friend Sara Delano also got married that month, to James Roosevelt from a distant part of the clan up on the Hudson River (see Roosevelt Family Tree, page 135). In 1882, they had a son, Franklin. Later on, when Elliott was visiting Sara and James, he met Anna Hall. Theodore was best man when Elliott and Anna married in 1883. A year later they had a daughter, and Theodore had his first niece: Anna Eleanor Roosevelt. One day, she'd be the world-famous First Lady, wife of the 32nd President, Franklin Delano Roosevelt, son of Sara Delano and old "Squire James."

THE GOVERNING CLASS

THEODORE AND ALICE MOVED INTO MITTIE'S BIG HOUSE on 57th Street. Every morning Theodore walked to his classes at Columbia Law School. He read and researched through the afternoons, then

1871

Oct. 8-14 —
Chicago Fire! 300 people die and 90,000 are homeless. Some say a cow's kick at a lantern started the flames.

1872

Thomas Adams *of Staten Island, NY, invents sticks of chewing gum.*

Mar. 1 —
The U.S. Congress establishes Yellowstone National Park.

May 10 —
Stockbroker **Victoria Claflin Woodhull** *becomes the first woman to run for the Presidency.* **Frederick Douglass** *is her running mate on the Equal Rights Party ticket.*

bathed and dressed for evenings at glittering dinner tables, theatres, and ballrooms with pretty Alice and New York's elite. Chances are, a few well-bred eyebrows lifted as this bunch got a load of young Mr. Roosevelt's other life: Theodore was flirting with politics.

Everybody knew that politics was a dirty business, full of bribery and strong-arm tactics behind the scenes. Bigshots at the top of the game ran for office so they could get rich and hand out cushy civil service jobs to their buddies. The "spoils system" – that's what people called the rough way things worked. In 1880, when Theodore first looked into getting into politics, he got himself laughed at. At the ground level, keeping the political machine running was grubby work generally done by horse-car conductors and saloonkeepers. It was no work for a gentleman – certainly not an eccentric, bespectacled, dressed up dude like Theodore Roosevelt!

Well, it hadn't been all that long since Theodore, Sr., the most gentle of gentlemen, had gotten entangled in politics. President Hayes wanted to clean up the government, so he tried but failed to put well-respected Thee into a job famous for its corruption: New York's customs collector. Thee was caught smack in the middle of a huge Republican fight between the President and powerful men who liked things just the way they were.

1872

July 4 –
Calvin Coolidge,
*future President, is
born in Vermont.*

*Nov. 5 –
Suffrage activist*
**Susan B.
Anthony,** U.S.
*citizen, is arrested
for voting in
Rochester, NY.*

*No longer will cattle roam the
West's open range thanks to*
Joseph Glidden's *new
invention: barbed wire.*

San Francisco – **Andrew S.
Hallidie** *invents the cable car.*

APPLIED IDEALISM

Americans in the last years of the 19th century could see progress as plain as day. On a train going faster than any horse could run, a person could ride from the Atlantic to the Pacific Ocean. Words crackled over telephone and telegraph wires, and Mr. Edison's light bulb could turn darkness into day. Folks couldn't help believing that all American life could be improved. Progress was only natural, but you had to work for it. Social workers such as Jane Addams opened settlement houses where immigrant families could find help getting established. W. E. B. Du Bois and Booker T. Washington struggled to right the wrongs of racial prejudice. Ida Bell Wells-Barnett worked to end *lynching* (folks, mostly black, being tortured and killed by mobs of lawless citizens, mostly white). Frances Willard led the nation's fight against drinking alcohol, a big part of

Thee's son must have believed that the political struggle had contributed to his dad's sickness and death. So a young man brought up on tales of heroic fights against impossible odds waded into the fray to see what he could do and to see if he could hold his own in the "rough and tumble." He explained it this way: "I intended to be one of the governing class."

1873

1874

The financial "Panic of 1873" touches off three years of bad economic times.

Jules Verne *writes* Around the World in 80 Days (*see* Nov. 14, 1889).

After **Mary Outerbridge** *sees English folks playing tennis in Bermuda, she introduces Americans to the game.*

Midwestern governors offer aid to farmers wiped out by grasshopper invasions.

domestic violence and poverty. For 50 years, Susan B. Anthony and Elizabeth Cady Stanton tried to pry women's right to vote out of the government's tight fist. People such as Samuel Gompers and Mary "Mother" Jones tried to better the lives of men, women, and children working long, hard days in mines and factories. Meanwhile, Theodore Roosevelt and others tried to make the everyday conduct of government's business fairer and more efficient. TR called his efforts "applied idealism," a good name for the work of all of these social reformers.

He joined the 21st District Republican Association. Its poker-playing, tobacco-chewing members met in a room full of cigar smoke and brass spittoons, upstairs over a bar. The guys made fun of Theodore's *pince-nez* (pinch-nose) glasses. They rolled their eyes when he showed up in his formal evening clothes and silk top hat, but the politicians came to admire his friendly persistence.

1874

Gold in the Black Hills! Ignoring dangers and U.S. promises not to trespass on Sioux reservation land, prospectors rush to Dakota Territory.

July 4 —
James B. Eads's *mighty Mississippi River bridge opens in St. Louis, MO.*

Aug. 10 —
Herbert Hoover, *future U.S. President, is born in Iowa.*

Nov. 7 —
Cartoonist **Thomas Nast** *comes up with the Republicans' elephant symbol.*

They knew the value of an energetic young man who stood out and who had money, strong opinions, and his father's good and well-known name. And snobbish Theodore came to admire men from lower down on the social ladder, men such as Joseph Murray, an Irishman who once was a drummer boy in the Union Army. He helped Theodore, the aristocratic upstart, get started in politics. But wait, the newlyweds hadn't had their big honeymoon yet.

No sappy stuff, now. While they were in Europe, Theodore climbed the Matterhorn. At nearly 15,000 feet, it towered over the

Matterhorn Honeymoon

Swiss-Italian border. This was the Mount Everest accomplishment of the era and a big, dangerous deal – all the bigger for a young man who'd been told by his doctor that he should protect his heart and take things easy. Back home, for the second time in TR's life, an assassin's bullet mortally wounded the nation's President. When

1874

French painters, disrespected by powerful critics, stage an independent art show. Their style is called Impressionist, from one of **Claude Monet**'s *paintings, "Impression: Sunrise."*

Nov. 30 —
Winston Churchill, *future author and British prime minister, is born in England.*

1875

Mark Twain *publishes* The Adventures of Tom Sawyer.

Folks are riding high-wheeler bicycles.

James Garfield died in September 1881, his office fell to Vice President Chester Arthur, former New York customs collector, the job that had caused Thee and President Hayes so much trouble. The honeymooners returned to a still-shocked, still-sad America.

A few weeks later, 23-year-old Theodore was nominated to run for the state legislature, and he won the election that November. About his early career in politics he wrote, "I rose like a rocket."

Well, not at first. As usual, folks needed time to get used to Theodore. His big white teeth flashed and snapped as his mouth tried to keep up with his flying thoughts. The new kid in the Albany Assembly *had* to be noticed, so he kept shouting with his high-pitched voice and upper-class accent: "Mister Spee-kah! Mister Spee-kah!" Reporters couldn't help noticing the "young man with eyeglasses, English side whiskers." As for newspaper cartoonists, they'd have almost too much fun drawing Theodore.

His three terms in the legislature were an eye-opener for him, too. Like many Americans, Theodore was fearful of the forces that were stirring up the working class: union organizers and masses of poor immigrants vying for jobs. He was a conservative young man who tended to see things from the point of view of his wealthy background. He'd agree, for instance, that low

1875   **1876**

Jan. 14 —
Albert Schweitzer,
*future musician,
doctor, author, medical
missionary in Africa,
and Nobel Peace
Prize winner is born.*

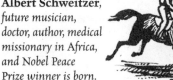

May 17 — Louisville, KY —
Aristedes *wins the first Kentucky Derby.*

Aug. 24 —
Matthew Webb, *27, is the first person to
swim across the English Channel: 21 miles
from Dover to Calais; 21 hours, 45 minutes.*

*Korea becomes
independent
from China.*

Young Mr. and Mrs. Roosevelt

taxes and cheap labor were good. If a law allowed streetcar conductors to work 12 instead of 15 hours per day, that'd mean the government was interfering with the free market and getting in the way of free citizens doing business as they pleased. Then, when Theodore was researching a labor law that would affect poor cigar makers, he saw whole families, most of them immigrants, working in crowded rooms beside their "foul bedding" and "scraps of food." For Theodore, it was a lesson. He knew that companies had to

1876

Mar. 7 —
Alexander Graham Bell *is issued a patent for his new invention: the telephone.*

A. G. BELL

Aug. 1 —
Colorado is the 38th state.

WILD BILL HICKOK

Aug. 2 —
Frontier scout and peace officer **James Butler "Wild Bill" Hickok** *is murdered in Deadwood, Dakota Territory.*

make money. And he came to know more clearly that people had to be able to live decently. Those needs had to be balanced.

Years later he'd remember what he saw in the tenements and write with great feeling about men who knew about law "but not life" and who blocked the path to fairness. He'd always try to find a proper balance between his beliefs and what he knew to be true in the world around him. All his political life he'd try to referee the conflict between big money and the common people, nature and humans, as well as his own sunny optimism and his dark despair.

Shadow

THEODORE HAD BEGUN RESEARCHING HIS FIRST BOOK, *The Naval War of 1812*, when he was in college. Not only was his book getting fine reviews, but Theodore also was making a name for himself in the state legislature. He and Alice moved into their

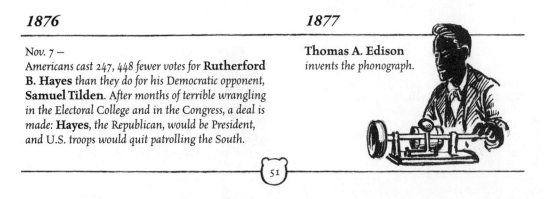

1876

Nov. 7 —
Americans cast 247, 448 fewer votes for **Rutherford B. Hayes** *than they do for his Democratic opponent,* **Samuel Tilden**. *After months of terrible wrangling in the Electoral College and in the Congress, a deal is made:* **Hayes**, *the Republican, would be President, and U.S. troops would quit patrolling the South.*

1877

Thomas A. Edison *invents the phonograph.*

own house at 55 West 45th Street, next door to newlyweds Corinne and Douglas Robinson. Out near Oyster Bay, Theodore had bought land for a farm and a big house to be called Leeholm, in honor of Alice's family name. Architects were planning its ten bedrooms and broad *piazza* (porch) where he and Alice would watch the sunset and their future kids running about.

Alice's husband decided to add to all of this happiness by going hunting. So it was that in the black and windy wee hours of a September morning in 1883, a lone Easterner stepped off a train in the Dakota Badlands. He'd come to the valley of the Little Missouri River with but one goal in mind – well, OK, two goals: He had to find a place to bunk for the night, and he sincerely wanted to hunt for however many buffalo might remain in what was left of the Wild West and kill one of them.

Don't think it was easy for him to hire someone to take a tenderfoot tourist out across the wild, weird landscape, but he finally did. Off they went, Theodore Roosevelt and his guide, Joe Ferris, through eight cold, hungry days complete with rain, rattlesnakes, and quicksand. Anyone else would call this miserable. Not Theodore! He had inherited his father's knack for finding joy in life.

1877

Canals on Mars? No, but people wonder after Italian astronomer **Giovanni Shiaparelli** *detects a series of lines on the planet's surface.*	**Anna Sewell** *writes* Black Beauty.	 CHIEF JOSEPH	*After the U.S. Government orders the Nez Perce off their land in Oregon,* **Chief Joseph** *tries to get them to Canada. He leads 800 people more than 1,000 miles before their final battle with U.S. troops — and their journey to Indian Territory in Oklahoma.*

Theodore's Badland buffalo celebration

"By Godfrey, but this is fun!" he cried. He was having a "bully" time of it, meaning ol' Theodore was having a blast.

Ferris stood astonished when, on the ninth day, ecstatic Theodore whooped, shouted, and danced around the buffalo he'd shot, then handed Ferris a $100 bonus. Soon Theodore was headed back East, envisioning the buffalo's stuffed head on his wall one day, proof of his skill as a hunter. On top of that, pretty Alice was waiting for him. And after the first of the year, she was going to have their baby. Who could be happier?

1877

Dec. 22 —
In New York City, the American Museum of Natural History opens to the public.

1878

Turkey is at war with Russia and with Greece.

Jan. 6 —
Poet-biographer **Carl Sandburg** is born in Illinois.

Jan. 9 —
King Victor Emmanuel II of Italy dies. His son, **Umberto I**, will take over.

On the cold night of February 12, 1884, in the big house on 57th Street, Bamie, Aunt Anna, and Corinne were looking after Mittie, who was sick in bed, and Alice, who was having a baby girl. Up in Albany, Theodore received the news about Alice. The delighted new dad hurried through last minute business. He was accepting congratulations from fellows puffing the cigars he'd passed around and getting ready to hurry home when a second telegram was brought to him.

Cold and dark on 57th Street

Six years. That's how long it had been since Theodore sat on another train, powerless to make it go any faster, then arrived home too late to say good-bye to his beloved dad. All around him was the gloomy sort of freezing fog that made folks shiver and turn up their coat collars. Late on Wednesday, February 13, Theodore finally exploded out of the carriage that had brought him from the station to the house on 57th Street. Elliott met him on the steps.

1878

The people of Deadwood, Dakota Territory, are deathly ill with smallpox. **Martha "Calamity Jane" Canary** *becomes a hero, taking care of sick folks night after night, day after day.*

1879

London, England — **Sir William Gilbert** and **Sir Arthur Sullivan** *present their operetta, H.M.S. Pinafore.*

Thomas A. Edison *perfects an electric light bulb.*

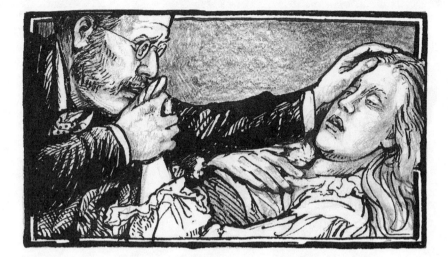

The light goes out.

"There's a curse on this house," he said. "Mother is dying and Alice is dying, too!"

The words proved hideously true. Typhoid fever took the life of 48-year-old Mittie Roosevelt at 3:00 a.m. Meanwhile, upstairs, an undetected childbirth complication was shutting down Alice's kidneys and killing her. At 2 p.m., 22-year-old Alice Lee Roosevelt died in Theodore's arms. In his diary for February 14, 1884, there's an **X**. Under it are these words: "The light has gone out of my life."

1879

British troops in South Africa conquer Zulu tribesmen in bloody fighting.

1880

Auguste Rodin *sculpts "The Thinker."*

Lew Wallace *writes* Ben Hur.

France colonizes the African Congo and annexes the island of Tahiti.

June 27 —
Helen Keller *is born in Alabama (see 1903).*

The Colonel's "crowded hour"

CHAPTER THREE

The Crowded Years 1884–1898

RIDING FASTER THAN SORROW

AT THE DOUBLE FUNERAL, people must have wondered how frozen-faced Theodore could stand such a loss. He named his daughter Alice Lee but called her "Baby Lee," unable at first to speak the word "Alice." Never did he talk about his wife, not even to her child. No diary pages full of grief this time. He closed himself up tight, left his baby with Bamie, and fled to Albany, where he worked hard and refused any sympathy. When the legislature closed and the noisy Republican convention was over out in Chicago, he headed back to Dakota. Theodore made himself stand

1881

Clara Barton *becomes the first president of the American Red Cross.*

Booker T. Washington *founds a school, now known as Tuskegee University, for African-American students.*

Mar. 13 — **Czar Alexander II** *of Russia is mortally wounded by an assassin's bomb.*

the loss he'd suffered. His famous smile and joy in living would be genuine and true. That doesn't mean that he ever got over what happened on Valentine's Day, 1884. Behind a locked door in his heart would always be his first love and the day he lost her.

Years away, in 1913, Theodore wrote nothing about Alice in his autobiography, but knowing the story of his life, you can imagine her there between the lines as he wrote about his years in the old frontier. "That land of the West is gone now, 'gone, gone with lost Atlantis', gone to the isle of ghosts and of strange dead memories. It was a land of vast silent spaces, of lonely rivers. . . ." In other words, it was a perfect place for romantic, devastated Theodore.

He'd always been one to test himself, and the West was a perfect place for that. And in the 1880s, he certainly wasn't the only one hoping to make money there. How? By buying and selling cattle, all destined to be beef dinners back East. In the next few years, he'd invest more than $80,000 in his two cattle ranches, the Elkhorn and the Chimney Butte (pronounced "byoot").

Theodore distracted himself and boosted his confidence by dressing up in just the right outfit. Chaps. Alligator hide boots. Sombrero. Silk neckerchief and fringed buckskin shirt. He felt he could face anything with his Winchester rifle, pearl-handled

---

1881

1882

July 15 —
New Mexico Territory —
Sheriff Pat Garrett
*shoots and kills
21-year-old serial killer*
William H. Bonney,
a.k.a. **Billy the Kid.**

Oct. 26 —
*Arizona Territory —
Tombstone's marshal,*
Virgil Earp, *his brother*
Wyatt, "Doc" Holliday,
*and others engage in a
shootout at the O.K. Corral.*

*Chinese folks have faced racism
and attacks for years in the U.S.,
mainly in the West. Now
Congress passes a law closing
the door to Chinese immigrants.
It won't be opened until 1943,
when China and the U.S. are
allies, battling Japan.*

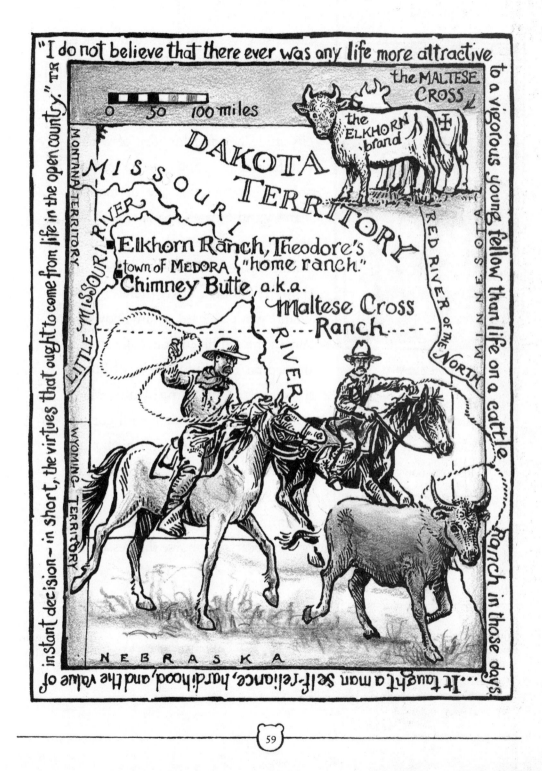

"I do not believe that there ever was any life more attractive to a vigorous young fellow than life on a cattle Ranch in those days. ...It taught a man self-reliance, hardihood, and the value of instant decision — in short, the virtues that ought to come from life in the open country." TR

the MALTESE CROSS

the ELKHORN brand

0   50   100 miles

DAKOTA TERRITORY

MONTANA TERRITORY

MISSOURI RIVER

LITTLE MISSOURI RIVER

RED RIVER OF THE NORTH

Elkhorn Ranch, Theodore's "home ranch."

town of MEDORA

Chimney Butte, a.k.a. Maltese Cross Ranch

MISSOURI RIVER

WYOMING TERRITORY

NEBRASKA

Theodore out West

revolver, silver spurs and belt buckle, and his hunting knife specially made at Tiffany's swanky jewelry store!

One look at this bespectacled city dude wearing his idea of what a tasteful rancher should wear considerably brightened the day of many a lean, wind-burned cowpoke. They about laughed themselves out of their saddles when Theodore called out, "hasten forward quickly there!" But he would work as hard as anybody and stay in the saddle 40 hours at a stretch if need be. He could laugh at himself, too, until a gun-toting drunk called him "Four-eyes" once too often, cussed too much, and got too close. Then a whole saloon full of men saw him put his boxing lessons to good use and deck the guy. As always, people learned not to underestimate Theodore Roosevelt.

He knew himself to be timid at heart. It could be scary dealing with cattle stampedes, grizzly bears, and horse thieves, but by

---

1882

Jan. 30 —
Franklin Delano Roosevelt, *future President, is born in New York.*

April 3 —
St. Joseph, MO —
Jesse James, *34, fugitive outlaw and folk hero, is murdered.*

Aug. 20 —
Moscow, Russia —
Peter Tchaikovsky's *1812 Overture is performed for the first time.*

New York — For the first time, a Christmas tree is decorated with electric lights.

acting as if he had courage, he "gradually ceased to be afraid." It was a good lesson. Here was another, one he'd learned when his dad died: "Black care rarely sits behind a rider whose pace is fast enough." He meant that sorrow wouldn't catch him if he kept on the move. If he stayed busy, despair wouldn't hang around.

Out in Dakota, pencil-necked, timid Teedie disappeared forever. The muscles in his neck and shoulders grew thick and hard, as he and the cowboys felt the "glory of work and the joy of living." Theodore fulfilled his solemn, long-ago promise to his father. He made his body into that of a barrel-chested man full of vitality and confirmed his belief in what Theodore called the "*strenuous* (energetic) life."

In his spare time he read and wrote books and made more than one trip back East. So his political buddies wouldn't forget him, he supported Republican James Blaine in the nation's 1884 Presidential campaign. (Democrat Grover Cleveland won it.) Theodore and his Long Island neighbors went fox hunting in the aristocratic British manner. He visited with Bamie and Baby Lee at the big new house he and Alice had planned. It was finished.

It was on one of these visits that Theodore ran into a childhood friend. No one but the two of them knew how it was that

1883

Robert Louis Stevenson *publishes* Treasure Island.

Carlo Collodi, (*a.k.a.* **Carlo Lorenzini**) *publishes* The Adventures of Pinocchio.

Ex-Pony Express rider, scout, buffalo-hunter **William F. Cody** *begins his Wild West Circus, known around the world as Buffalo Bill's Wild West Show.*

they came to love each other over the next months, but they did. Some said that book-loving Edith Carow had always been sweet on Conie Roosevelt's big brother. On November 17, 1885, no one but Edith and Theodore knew that they were engaged, but they were.

In the strict society of New York's upper class, the fact that Alice had been dead less than two years could cause mean gossip. It troubled Theodore, too. He didn't want to seem faithless to Alice up in heaven, or to hurt her. It was something he had to work out while Edith was off in Europe and he rode and roped in Dakota.

As usual, he kept himself busy. He tracked down a trio of hard-luck boat thieves and made sure he got his picture taken with them when he brought them to justice. He wrote a book. Then, back home, he tried but failed to become mayor of New York City – all this before 28-year-old Theodore and Edith, 25, were married on a thick gray day in London, December 2, 1886.

Meanwhile, out in America's plains and prairies, thousands of cattle huddled together, freezing and starving in the icy blizzards of the killer winter of 1886 - 1887. When the snows finally melted, their bones were scattered across the land. The poor beasts were done forever with the ranching business. So was Theodore, though he would never be done with the West.

1883   **1884**

May 24 —
After 14 years of
dangerous work,
the Brooklyn
Bridge, designed by
John Augustus
Roebling, *is open.*

Aug. 24 —
More than 36,000
people die when the
volcano Krakatoa
erupts in Indonesia.
Folks 3,000 miles away
hear the explosion.

Great Britain —
Mark Twain *publishes*
The Adventures of
Huckleberry Finn.
(It will be published
next year in the U.S.)

SAGAMORE HILL

THEODORE AND EDITH SETTLED INTO THE BIG HOUSE once known as Leeholm. Now it was called Sagamore Hill, named after an Abenaki *sagamore* (chief) whose people once lived thereabouts.

The grownups decided that three-year-old Alice, despite her tears, would leave Aunt Bamie and live instead with Theodore, Edith, and in 1887, baby Theodore, Jr., "a howling polly parrot" in his big sister's opinion. She and her father became better acquainted. He gave excellent piggyback rides, she discovered.

Eventually, the Roosevelts filled Sagamore Hill with thousands of books and many a hunting trophy, pale tusks, and antlers. The skins of polar bear, zebra, leopard, lion, and grizzly bear were rugs beneath their feet. Theodore proudly used a waste basket made from an elephant's foot and dipped his pen into a rhinoceros-foot inkwell. Nearly 20 calm-faced, glass-eyed animal

1884

| Bolivia becomes a landlocked nation when a war is settled between Chile and Peru. | May 8 — **Harry S. Truman,** future President, is born in Missouri. | May 19 — Baraboo, Wisconsin — First performance of the circus begun by the **Ringling Brothers**, Albert, Otto, Alfred, Charles, and John. Two other brothers, August and Henry, join later on. |

heads – moose, musk ox, bison, and antelopes among others – loomed over a house full of six young Roosevelts: Alice, Ted, then Kermit in 1889, and Ethel in 1891, a "jolly, naughty, whacky baby,"

The happy young Roosevelt family.

said her father. Archibald (better known as Archie) was born in 1894 and, in 1897, Quentin, the baby of the family.

Much of the money he'd inherited was lost when his cattle froze to death, so Theodore, the "literary feller," devoted himself

1884

Oct. 11 –
Eleanor Roosevelt, *future First Lady, is born in New York City.*

Nov. 4 –
Grover Cleveland *is elected 22nd U.S. President.*

1885

One last act of courage: As he's dying of cancer, ex-President **Ulysses S. Grant** *writes his memoir.* **Mark Twain** *will see that it is published.*

Louis Pasteur *develops a rabies vaccine.*

LOUIS PASTEUR

to writing books, including a multi-volume history of the West, to support his growing family.

With the 1889 inauguration of a Republican President, Benjamin Harrison, Theodore went to Washington as one of three Civil Service Commissioners. He'd be making sure that folks in the post office and other government workers had their jobs because they could do them, not because a politician owed someone a favor. Theodore's job, which he got because of his own political connections, was to find corruption and root it out. He did both and opened up more government posts for women, too.

While her father was at work, little Alice Roosevelt loved galloping around Washington's parks, pretending to be "a fiery horse, preferably cream-colored" that could suddenly turn into a "princess with very long hair." In the afternoons, she, Ted, and Kermit waited for their dad at the corner of Farragut Square to walk home. Long-gone Thee used to bring toys to Bamie, Teedie, Ellie, and Conie. Now Theodore brought presents for his own children: toy horses and cows, carefully branded with a hot hairpin. Alice's Uncle Elliott and his family weren't nearly so happy. Two years after illness killed his wife and son, Elliott died in 1894 from too much drinking, when Alice was ten. Her father and her

1885

Both **Gottlieb Daimler** and **Karl Benz** *come up with successful gasoline engines. Gottlieb uses his to build the first real motorcycle. Karl puts his in a wheeled carriage: the first automobile.*

Englishman **J. K. Starley** *manufactures the first commercially successful "safety" bike, a bicycle with same-size wheels.*

aunts, Bamie and Corinne, were shattered. Alice's cousins, Eleanor Roosevelt and little brother, Hall, were sent to live with their dead mom's strict, gloomy mother.

The Roosevelt family left Washington in the spring of 1895 when restless, ambitious Theodore accepted a chance to work on New York City's Police Commission. In short order, he encouraged the corrupt Chief of Police to step down and broke old barriers when he hired a woman to be his secretary. He started a police bicycle squad as well as a marksmanship school (the beginning of New York's police academy) and stirred up a hot ruckus when he began enforcing the law against saloons being open on Sundays. His efforts pushed his personal star ever higher in the sky of national politics. In his rare spare time, he campaigned for William McKinley, an Ohio Republican running against William Jennings Bryan in 1896 in one of the most exciting presidential campaigns ever. Theodore injected his views on U.S. foreign policy into his speeches: The U.S. should drive the Spanish out of Cuba! The country needed a stronger navy!

People might not agree with his opinions, but they sure liked the emphatic way he said them. Reporters wrote about Teddy (a nickname that Theodore came to find annoying), the

---

1885

Amazing sharpshooter **Annie Oakley** *joins Buffalo Bill's Wild West Show.*

June 17 —
France's gift to the American people, **Frederic Auguste Bartholdi's** *"Statue of Liberty," arrives in New York City.*

July 1 —
King Leopold II *of Belgium establishes a colony in the Congo (present-day Zaire) so he can plunder its rubber, copper, and other resources. Many Africans died under the Belgians' cruel treatment.*

way he wrapped himself in a black cape, black hat pulled low, prowling the streets by night, looking for policemen goofing off or sleeping on duty. Cartoonists drew the Teddy combo: glasses,

Theodore in New York City

grin, and moustache. Vendors sold whistles shaped like their name: "Teddy's Teeth."

After McKinley was elected President, he let himself be talked into giving Theodore a much-desired position back in the nation's capital: Assistant Secretary of the Navy. Once again the Roosevelts were on their way to Washington. Now Theodore *really* stirred things up.

1886

Robert Louis Stevenson *writes* The Strange Case of Dr. Jekyll and Mr. Hyde.

May 4 —
Labor movement turns deadly. Chicago's Haymarket Square is filled with people striking for an 8-hour workday when an unknown someone throws a bomb, killing 8 policemen and wounding 67. Many workers are killed when police charge into the mob, guns blazing (see Nov. 11, 1887).

GONE TO BE A SOLDIER

AT FIRST, JOHN D. LONG, SECRETARY OF THE NAVY, was pleased to have such a smart go-getter for an assistant, one with such firm ideas about America's Navy. For one thing, it needed more battle-ships, THE main weapons in this pre-airplane time. Germany, Austria-Hungary, France, Russia, Great Britain, and Japan were building up their navies. Theodore saw, long before his fellow citizens did, that the U.S. would be a major player on the world's stage, and that meant being a power at sea. He believed that whether you were a nation or a person, whether you were fighting or keeping the peace, you had to be strong. Only then could you distinguish yourself in battle, and it was in battle where glory was to be had. "No triumph of peace is quite so great," Theodore exclaimed, "as the supreme triumphs of war."

When he gave speeches, saber-rattling Theodore grumbled

1886

June 3 —
Grover Cleveland, *the only President to get married in the White House, is wed to* **Frances Folsom.**

Sept. 4 —
After years of fighting on the Mexican border, U.S. troops capture Apache warrior **Geronimo.**

Geronimo

Atlanta pharmacist **John S. Pemberton** *invents a headache remedy and calls it Coca-Cola.*

about Spain's presence in nearby Cuba and Puerto Rico. In fact, Cubans were trying to rid themselves of their Spanish rulers. When Japan growled about U.S. presence in Hawaii, he did not hide his anger. If America wished to take over territory, it didn't need any foreign power's permission or approval! This was hot stuff coming from Theodore, a government official. It sounded like he wanted the U.S. to grab lands beyond her shores, to behave as if America were an empire. Not everybody agreed with Theodore. He made some people nervous.

Summer at Sagamore Hill

As summer settled on Washington, Theodore headed up to Sagamore Hill to swim, boat, picnic, and ride with his "bunnies," his name for his children. They scrambled through the woods and splashed across streams as he led them on nature walks.

1887   **1888**

Dreadful blizzards are howling over the Great Plains.

Arthur Conan Doyle publishes A Study in Scarlet, introducing the world to great detective **Sherlock Holmes.**

Sherlock Holmes

Nov. 11 — With no proof of guilt, four anarchists are hanged for the deaths in Haymarket Square (see May 4, 1886).

Six women are killed in London, England, by the mysterious **Jack the Ripper.**

SILVER AND GOLD AND THE POPULIST TORNADO

The United States had become a great industrial power, but its factory workers were hardly paid enough to feed their families. Dirt-poor miners dug a wealth of ore and coal out of the earth. Despite hard work and fertile land, farmers were going broke. Why? Low crop prices and the high cost of bank loans and of getting their crops to market on the train. In 1890, 11 million of America's 12 million families lived on an average income of less than $400 a year. Even little kids were putting in long, hard hours working alongside their parents. So where was the money? Invested in banks, railroads, mines, mills, and such that kept the wheels of business turning, and it was deep in the pockets of a wealthy few.

Every dollar anyone had was backed with gold in the U.S. Treasury. The rich tended to support this "gold standard." Those with less wanted the government to print and mint more money, backed with cheaper silver. It wouldn't be worth as much, but at least poorer folks would have more of it. This money battle was part of a political storm that blew across the land in the last part of the 19th century.

Mary E. Lease of Kansas, the "Patrick Henry in Petticoats," fired folks up with hot speeches. "What you farmers need," she cried, "is to raise less corn and more hell!" Rural folks formed a Farmers' Alliance, then, in 1891, linked up with other activists to create the People's Party, a.k.a. the *Populists*. From state houses to the U.S. Congress, the Populist tornado blew legislators and governors out of and into office. It scared conservative politicians and businessmen, who didn't want things to change, just about half to death. They poured fortunes into presidential campaigns, defeating the Populist-leaning William Jennings Bryan in 1896, 1900, then again in 1908.

What did the Populists want? In 1892, they called for the government to take over the railroads, telephone, and telegraph companies. (To their conservative opponents, this sounded like plain old communism and warfare between the social classes straight out of Russia!) More direct elections in which folks could introduce and vote on laws, an 8-hour workday instead of the usual 12, equal opportunities, and social justice. The People's Party faded away in 1908 as mainstream politicians, Theodore Roosevelt and Woodrow Wilson for instance, championed these "progressive" goals. Many of them became reality in the hard 1930s, during the Presidency of TR's cousin, Franklin D. Roosevelt (husband of Elliott's daughter, Eleanor). Those Populist ideas still blow in the wind, here in the dark and stormy 21st century.

Evenings were for reading aloud or telling ghost stories, Theodore's specialty. Then he hurried away for more fun: running the Navy while his boss was still on vacation.

Nights cooled, leaves fell, and fall turned into winter. According to news reports, cruel Spanish officials were herding the families of Cuban rebels into camps. Far off in the South Pacific, they were struggling to control the islanders of the Philippines. (These islands, handily located near Indonesia, China, and increasingly powerful Japan, were highly prized by strategic thinkers such as Theodore.) The old Spanish Empire was crumbling. In America, big-time publishers William Randolph Hearst and Joseph Pulitzer were printing sensational stories about bloody Spanish cruelties because they wanted to 1) Make Americans angry, and 2) Sell newspapers.

Remember the Maine!

1888

| January — Washington, DC — The National Geographic Society is formed. | *Mar. 11 – 14 — Hundreds of people and horses die when the northeastern U.S. is blizzard-blasted.* | *Oct. 9 — The finished Washington Monument opens to the public.* | | *Nov. 6 —* **Grover Cleveland** *is defeated.* **Benjamin Harrison** *is elected 23rd President.* |

In January 1898, when Theodore and Edith's new baby Quentin was two months old, President McKinley sent a battleship to Havana, Cuba, to show that the U.S. was keeping an eye on things. Out in the glassy harbor on the night of February 15, 1898, U.S. sailors were minding their own – and Cuba's – business when the USS *Maine* exploded, killing more than 260 men.

Newspaper headlines screamed, "Remember the *Maine!*" Nowadays, it's thought that an accident in one of the *Maine's* coalbunkers caused the blowup. Back then, though, Theodore was sure that Spain did the dastardly deed and should be paid back with war! When the President insisted upon a lengthy investigation, Theodore snapped that McKinley had "the backbone of a chocolate éclair!" In fact, William McKinley had seen plenty of death in the Civil War and wasn't eager to send men to battle.

Theodore was even more agitated by dangers at home. Edith was very sick with a tumor in her abdomen. Surgeons saved her, but weeks passed before she was strong again. And poor ten-year-old Ted was suffering with headaches. Imagine how badly TR felt when doctors found that the little boy was cracking under his dad's high expectations. Never again, he promised, would he pressure Ted. He'd direct his energies at the Navy instead.

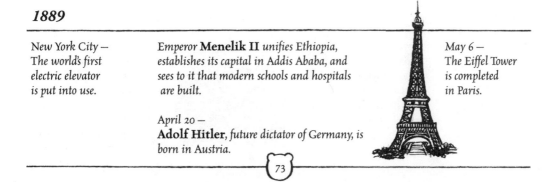

1889

New York City — The world's first electric elevator is put into use.

Emperor **Menelik II** *unifies Ethiopia, establishes its capital in Addis Ababa, and sees to it that modern schools and hospitals are built.*

April 20 — **Adolf Hitler,** *future dictator of Germany, is born in Austria.*

May 6 — *The Eiffel Tower is completed in Paris.*

He was so convinced that the U.S. was on the brink of a necessary war that he did all he could to push it over the edge.

On February 25, when his boss was away, Theodore ordered more fuel, manpower, and Commodore George Dewey to be ready, with his six warships, to strike at the Spanish fleet in the Philippine Islands. However upset they were at Theodore's boldness, both Secretary Long and President McKinley allowed his actions to stand. Thus, Dewey's ships were in place when McKinley declared war on Spain. They wiped out all ten of the ships Spain had near the Philippines on May 1, 1898. The U.S. won the first major battle of the Spanish-American War.

Theodore had a small, significant role in that victory all right, but he wanted to do more, never mind his age (39), his eyes (weak), a new baby plus five other children at home, a wife still frail from illness. Never mind that people thought he was nuts. For weeks he'd been bugging every official he knew to allow him to go to war.

Personally and politically, it would be shameful, Theodore figured, if he didn't practice what he'd been preaching. It was a chance "to cut my little notch on the stick that stands as a measuring-rod in every family." He'd do what his father didn't do in 1861: test himself in battle as a soldier. To grab this chance at

1889

May 31 —
In Pennsylvania, the Johnstown Flood kills as many as 5,000 people.

April 22 —
At the crack of a pistol shot, 50,000 people rush to claim parts of Oklahoma for themselves in newly opened Indian Territory.

Nov. 2 —
North Dakota is the 39th state; South Dakota is the 40th.

Nov. 8 —
Montana is the 41st state.

destiny, so he said later, he'd have turned from his wife's deathbed. Lucky for him and Edith, it didn't come to that. She was feeling well enough to know how painful it'd be for everyone if Theodore stayed home. She gave him her blessings.

He quit his job, ordered a snappy tailored uniform, tucked 12 spare pairs of steel-rimmed glasses into his bags, kissed his wife and "bunnies" good-bye (perhaps forever), and rode away on May 12, 1898. The chief adventure of Theodore Roosevelt's adventurous life had begun.

Colonel Wood and Lieutenant Colonel Roosevelt

Colonel Leonard Wood, an army surgeon, would lead; Theodore would be second in command of the First U.S. Volunteer Cavalry.

1889

Nov. 14 —
Reporter **Nellie Bly** (*a.k.a.* **Elizabeth Cochrane**) *is determined to outdo the hero of* **Jules Verne**'s *1873 novel* Around the World in 80 Days. *By ship, train, and stagecoach, Nellie circles the globe in 72 days, 6 hours, and 11 minutes, returning on Jan. 25, 1890.*

Dec. 6 —
Ex-president of the Confederacy **Jefferson Davis** *is dead at 81.*

THE ROUGH RIDERS

WHEN WORD GOT OUT THAT THEODORE WAS GOING TO WAR, thousands of men signed up to be one of "Teddy's Tigers" or "Teddy's Texas Tarantulas" – about 20,000 too many for one regiment, however it was nicknamed. The chosen, nearly 1,250 men, gathered at San Antonio, Texas. Most were weather-beaten cowboys and farmhands from the Southwest and Indian Territory. Along with athletes from eastern colleges, champion tennis and polo players, society clubmen, New York cops, and a pair of Englishmen, they'd be forever known as "Roosevelt's Rough Riders."

Horses and riders both learned military ways out in the heat and the dust. Deep voices chanted, "Rough, rough, we're the stuff! We want to fight, and we can't get enough! Whoopee!"

They were eager to get to the action. "The sooner the better," Theodore wrote in his letter to the President. It's easy to picture

---

1890

Theodore's friend **Jacob Riis** becomes America's first photojournalist with his report and shocking photographs of New York City's slums in his book How the Other Half Lives.

Illustrator **Charles Dana Gibson** publishes the first of hundreds of drawings of his ideal American beauty: the famous Gibson Girl.

July 3 — Idaho is the 43rd state.

July 10 — Wyoming is the 44th state.

a corner of McKinley's mouth turning up. The sunburned Riders whooped with delight and belted out their favorite song, "There'll Be a Hot Time in the Old Town Tonight!" when they were ordered off to Florida and then to a "destination unknown."

After a day spent coaxing 1,200 mules and horses into boxcars, the men slept by the tracks until their own train showed up early on May 30. At stops along the way, folks waited with cheers, cold watermelon, and beer for the hot, miserable soldiers. Three days

Rough-riding their way to war

on the rails took them to Tampa, a city of corrals, horses, tents, flies, and mosquitoes. Officers and reporters stayed at a fancy hotel with porches full of rocking chairs. Edith Roosevelt stayed there, too. She'd come south to be with Theodore before he shipped out.

That didn't happen until after almost a week of confusion, military parades, and a disappointing double whammy for the

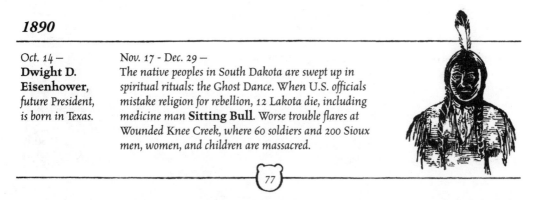

1890

Oct. 14 —
Dwight D. Eisenhower, *future President, is born in Texas.*

Nov. 17 - Dec. 29 —
The native peoples in South Dakota are swept up in spiritual rituals: the Ghost Dance. When U.S. officials mistake religion for rebellion, 12 Lakota die, including medicine man **Sitting Bull**. *Worse trouble flares at Wounded Knee Creek, where 60 soldiers and 200 Sioux men, women, and children are massacred.*

Rough Riders: Only 560 of the men could go, and only the officers could bring their horses. A hard business it was to tell this news. Strong men wept when they heard they had to stay behind.

A huge, tangled job it was, moving horses, equipment, and more than 15,000 men from camp to the ships. The Riders' train didn't show up, so they talked their way onto a coal train. It was aimed the wrong way, so backward down the track they went, to Tampa's madhouse of a seaport. After a long wait and a last-minute scramble, Theodore and the men, caked black with sweat and coal dust, hurried onto an overbooked transport ship.

Now they were on their way, right? Wrong. Word of unidentified warships in the Gulf of Mexico stopped the armada. Hot sun. Steel ships. Six days. Below decks, animals died. Men simmered like pigeons in a pot. At last, on June 14, 1898, the flotilla was underway.

U.S. sailors had been blockading and bombarding Cuba's coast, making it safe for soldiers' landing, but they couldn't tame the sea. Soldiers fought through wild water to get ashore. Some horses were lowered into the waves in slings, but most of the terrified animals were simply shoved overboard to swim to shore as best they could. A huge wave washed over one of

---

1891

Thomas A. Edison *invents a moving-picture camera.*

"Pike's Peak or Bust" is lettered on many a wagon cover as goldseekers rush west to Colorado. "In God we trusted. In Kansas we busted." These words might be seen on the eastbound wagons of thousands of Kansans defeated by drought and the high cost of farming.

Springfield, MA — P. E. *teacher* **James A. Naismith** *invents basketball.*

Theodore's horses and drowned her. He and his other horse, Texas, and the dripping Rough Riders struggled to the shore. Much of their baggage never made it off the boat. Theodore did have his gun and ammunition belt, sword, toothbrush, and his yellow raincoat. He managed to keep his hat on, and a good thing, too. He had tucked extra pairs of glasses in the lining.

The soldiers' mission, in part, was to take Santiago de Cuba away from the Spaniards. Between them and this seaport lay miles of mountainous jungle, slithering with snakes and buzzing with bugs. Regular soldiers, meaning the military was their career, tramped through the rain along with the volunteer Rough Riders

Wood's Weary Walkers

(a.k.a. Wood's Weary Walkers), war correspondents Richard Harding Davis and Stephen Crane, author of a famous 1895 novel, *The Red Badge of Courage*. Theodore marched too, refusing to ride while his men walked.

1892

Ida Bell Wells-Barnett, *journalist, begins her long campaign to end America's nasty, all-too-common practice of lynching.*

Peter Tchaikovsky *composes* The Nutcracker *ballet.*

April 19 — *Charles and J. Frank,* **the Duryea brothers,** *build one of America's very first automobiles.*

Before the shooting began on June 24, Theodore heard strange birdcalls: Snipers' signals, it turned out. Bullets whirred out of the jungle and thudded into men. At first, Theodore had an awful time knowing just what to do. Still, as he wrote, "one learns fast in a fight." He and some of the troops plunged through the jungle to a point where they could fire on the dug-in Spaniards. Then all of the men combined in a charge that drove more than a thousand of the enemy running from their mountain strongholds. After this Battle of Las Guasimas, Theodore picked up three empty Spanish cartridges for his children. For the family honor, he'd proven himself under fire.

Great day of the wolf

1892

June 29 — Homestead, PA —
Metal workers strike for decent pay.
Andrew Carnegie's *steel company hires 300 tough Pinkerton guards to end the strike and break the union. Four deaths and hundreds of injuries later, men go back to work for the same old pay.*

Nov. 8 —
Grover Cleveland
is reelected President.

1893

Wealthy sugar and pineapple planters force **Queen Liliuokalani** *from her throne, a first step to Hawaii's becoming a U.S. territory (see June 14, 1900).*

When Leonard Wood took over for a general sick with fever, Colonel Theodore Roosevelt took command of the Rough Riders. They joined in the massive attack on Santiago on July 1, 1898, and earned permanent national fame. Intense, thundering, bloody fighting in 100-degree weather, but for Theodore it was sublime, "the great day of my life." The best way he could describe the fierce joy of that day was "a wolf rising" in his heart.

All of his huge will was focused. Men followed purely confident, courageous Theodore through blood-red streams clogged with shattered bodies. Astride Texas, he rode among and beside his men and soldiers from other units, black and white. He encouraged and yelled at them as they charged up, up, up through tall grass and blazing gunfire to the top of hotly defended Kettle Hill, Theodore in the lead. When the Spaniards fled, running, shouting Theodore and all who were still able repeated their astonishing performance on nearby San Juan Hill. Below them lay Santiago de Cuba. U.S. soldiers and sailors had it surrounded. After days of sweaty, sickening siege, the seaport's defenders surrendered on July 17.

About a week later, the U.S. took over Puerto Rico. On August 13, U.S. troops took Manila, main seaport of the Philippines.

1893

Whitcomb L. Judson *invents what will be known as the zipper.*

Chicago fair-goers at the World's Columbian Exposition ride engineer **George Ferris's** *huge— 250 feet in diameter!— "pleasure wheel."*

Social worker **Lillian Wald** *begins New York City's Henry Street Settlement House. Like Chicago's Hull House, founded in 1889 by* **Jane Addams** *and* **Ellen Starr***, its mission is providing child care, classes, and such to new immigrants.*

righteousness...our whole national history has been one of expansion...

"Every expansion of a great civilized power means a victory for law, order and

AMERICAN EMPIRE
AND THE SPLENDID LITTLE WAR

On December 10, 1898, diplomats signed the treaty ending the Spanish-American War, "a splendid little war," according to John Hay, U.S. Secretary of War. It had lasted 113 days. Nearly 60,000 men died, including some 3,500 Americans, mostly from tropical diseases. Americans were proud of victory over once-mighty Spain, but many, then as now, disliked getting entangled with countries beyond U.S. shores. In 1796, George Washington himself had warned, "Have with [foreign Nations] as little political connection as possible." Of course the world was very different then.

When, in 1899, the U.S. Senate ratified the treaty (by one vote), the island of Puerto Rico (first settled by Spaniards in 1508) and the island of Guam (Spain's since 1561) became U.S. territory. The Philippine Islands were named after Spanish King Philip II back in 1565. Now, after a $20 million payment to Spain, they, too, would belong to the U.S. along with land fought and bled over, bought and/or stolen from Native Americans, French, Russians, English, Hawaiians, and Mexicans in the previous centuries. The U.S. poured money into the Philippines for roads, harbors, education, sanitation, baseball, and civil government headed by Ohio judge William Howard Taft. After about three years of cruel, deadly guerrilla war, America's "little brown brothers," as Taft termed the Filipinos, settled into their new status as residents of a territory in the American Empire.

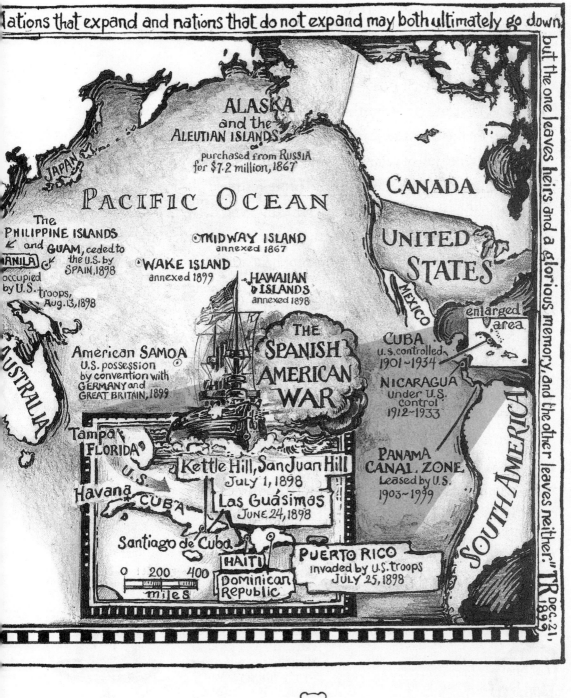

ations that expand and nations that do not expand may both ultimately go down.

but the one leaves heirs and a glorious memory, and the other leaves neither." TR Dec. 21, 1899

JAPAN

ALASKA
and the
ALEUTIAN ISLANDS
purchased from RUSSIA
for $7.2 million, 1867

PACIFIC OCEAN

CANADA

UNITED
STATES

The
PHILIPPINE ISLANDS
and GUAM, ceded to
the U.S. by
SPAIN, 1898

MANILA
occupied
by U.S.
troops,
Aug. 13, 1898

MIDWAY ISLAND
annexed 1867

WAKE ISLAND
annexed 1899

HAWAIIAN
ISLANDS
annexed 1898

MEXICO

enlarged
area

CUBA
U.S. controlled
1901~1934

American SAMOA
U.S. possession
by convention with
GERMANY and
GREAT BRITAIN, 1899

THE
SPANISH
AMERICAN
WAR

NICARAGUA
under U.S.
control
1912~1933

AUSTRALIA

Tampa,
FLORIDA

U.S.

Havana

CUBA

Kettle Hill, San Juan Hill
JULY 1, 1898

Las Guásimas
JUNE 24, 1898

PANAMA
CANAL ZONE
leased by U.S.
1903~1999

SOUTH AMERICA

Santiago de Cuba

0   200   400
miles

HAITI
Dominican
Republic

PUERTO RICO
invaded by U.S. troops
JULY 25, 1898

They didn't know that a truce had been signed the day before and that the Spanish-American War was pretty much over, but it had and it was. The Rough Riders' job was done.

One out of every three of these brave men was killed, wounded, or sick – mostly the latter. No other U.S. regiment in the Spanish- American War suffered as many casualties. Mosquitoes full of yellow fever or malaria took far more lives than enemy guns. None too gently, Theodore urged the not-so-efficient officials in Washington to bring him and his fever-wracked soldiers home. On August 8, their ship dropped anchor at the eastern tip of Long Island. Crowds of people, including comrades who'd been left behind in Florida, cheered for them and for their daredevil Colonel. He was a celebrity before he went to Cuba. Now, Teddy Roosevelt was the most famous man in America.

A few weeks later, the Riders pooled their money for a farewell present for Theodore. Tears glittered in his eyes when he saw it, a bronze "Bronco Buster," sculpted by the totally brilliant artist Frederic Remington. After 133 days, the official life of the First U.S. Volunteer Cavalry was over, but the Rough Riders would always be a part of Theodore Roosevelt's life, as he would be in theirs, until the end of all their days.

1893

Fall River, MA. At her sensational trial, **Lizzie Borden** *is found not guilty of ax-murdering her father and stepmother.*

English professor **Katharine Lee Bates** *writes "America the Beautiful."*

Kentucky sisters **Mildred** *and* **Patty Hill** *write a song for Mildred's kindergarten class: "Happy Birthday to You."*

LIKE A ROCKET

FROM HIS STIFF BROWN HAIR AND TANNED FACE down to his boots, Theodore radiated energy. It was as if a dynamo was whirring in that big chest of his. Behind his specs, his blue eyes squinted and glinted. Editors wanted to print Colonel Roosevelt's words. Newspaper people and curious "camera fiends" (Edith's term) lurked around her house, wanting pictures and information. When one asked five-year-old Archie where the Colonel might be, he said "I don't know where the Colonel is but Father is taking a bath."

Peppery Senator Tom Platt, big boss of New York politics, wasn't sure he wanted Theodore to be governor, but he very much wanted to elect a Republican, so he nominated the popular Hero of San Juan Hill. Across New York, at every stop of his flag-covered train, a Rough Rider sounded a bugle charge, and Theodore flashed his famous smile, smooched babies, and gave

1893   1894

May 5 —
A price drop on
Wall Street starts
a few years of
terrible economic
times in the U.S.

Rudyard
Kipling *writes*
The Jungle Book.

Mar. 25 —
Jacob S. Coxey *and hundreds of*
ragged, unemployed folks, "Coxey's
Army," start marching from Massillon,
Ohio, to Washington, D.C. Will the
President or any Congressmen see
them when they get there? No.

as many as 20 patriotic speeches a day to excited crowds. They elected him, then, up in Albany on the bitter, below-zero first Monday of 1899, he was sworn into office. Before long, Tom Platt's opinion of him was almost as cold as the weather. What had made him think he could control Theodore Roosevelt?

It wasn't so bad that Theodore met with reporters in his office every day, something no other governor had ever done. He used them to publicize his views, a tactic that his cousin Franklin Roosevelt would use with great success in his Presidency (1933-45). Theodore made laborers' lives a bit easier and safer, and he spoke out about the need to care for the wild, natural world. But when Theodore chose men for key jobs without his approval, Boss Platt fumed. Worse, Theodore pushed for a tax on public utility corporations that grew ever richer at the people's expense. It was an old greedy game: Corporations contributed to the political parties that elected men to the government who would protect corporations who contributed – well, you get the idea. Theodore wanted a fair balance between the needs of business on the one hand and the public good on the other. Platt wanted business-as-usual – not some radical reformer rocking the boat! He'd just as soon shove Theodore overboard – but how?

1894

May 11—
In Chicago, men who build Pullman railroad cars take a 25 percent pay cut but still have to live in pricey houses owned by wealthy **George Pullman**'s company. When the workers strike, sympathetic railroad men refuse to connect Pullman cars. Train traffic jams all over the Midwest.

July 3 —
President Cleveland orders U.S. troops to Chicago to end the railroad strike. Seven people die in the resulting violence.

Aug. 6—
Penniless Pullman workers give up the strike. A sorry chapter in U.S. history ends.

*"The twentieth century looms before us,
big with the fate of many nations."*
—TR April 10, 1899

Bonfires light up the night of New Year's Eve, 1899. The U.S. can boast 45 states; 677,000 telephones; 30,000 trolley cars; maybe 150 miles of paved roads; about 8,000 horseless carriages, such as Stanley Steamers, Duryea buggies, and Riker electrics; and countless vehicles drawn by mules or horses. America has perhaps 20,000 town bands and 76,094,000 citizens. This year, approximately 95,000 kids will graduate from high school and 450,000 immigrants will come to America, mostly from Europe. The average American worker makes 22 cents an hour and pays 12 cents for a dozen eggs. Coffee is 15 cents a pound; the same amount of beef or a can of corn or a drugstore ice-cream soda costs a dime. A ready-made man's suit costs $9.00, and work shoes are $1.25. A store-bought silk petticoat is 5 bucks, and this year ladies will buy $14 million dollars' worth of corsets. The Sears & Roebuck mail order catalogue offers a wooden ice box for only $8.95.

In Washington, D.C., a long line of citizens dressed in their best gathers outside the White House on the morning of New Year's Day, 1900, for the President's annual reception. They'll shake hands with William McKinley and bow to his wife, Ida.

Fate stepped in on November 21, 1899. McKinley's Vice President Garrett Hobart died.

If, in 1900, President McKinley took the Colonel on as his new running mate, he'd be out of Platt's hair. But Theodore agreed with John Adams. The very first Vice President called the VP job "the most insignificant office that ever the invention of man contrived." Both Theodore and McKinley needed convincing. As for Mark Hanna, the Republican chairman, he thought New York's young governor was nuts. In the end, after a lot of public ballyhoo and behind-the-scenes work by Platt and his buddies, the Colonel was on the ticket. While McKinley was quietly presidential, Theodore traveled 21,000 miles and made a thousand speeches prefaced by at least that many Rough Rider bugle calls. McKinley triumphed over his Democratic opponent, William Jennings Bryan, and as of March 4, 1901, Theodore was Vice President.

He figured that his quiet new job would give him time to hunt and be with his family. Not exactly.

Six months later, on September 6, 1901, William McKinley was visiting the Pan-American Exposition in Buffalo, New York, when Leon Czolgosz, an anarchist who wanted no part of any

1894   **1895**

Nov. 1 —
Czar Alexander III
dies. His 24-year-old son **Nicholas** *becomes Russia's absolute ruler (see July 16, 1918).*

W. E. B. Du Bois *is the first black student to earn and receive a Ph.D. degree at Harvard University.*

German physicist,
Wilhelm K. Roentgen
discovers X-rays. With them, doctors can see bones in a patient's body.

government, shot the President twice with a gun hidden beneath a handkerchief.

At first it looked like McKinley was improving, so Theodore left the President's bedside and went back to his holiday in the Adirondack Mountains. Urgent telegrams sent him rushing back. He arrived in Buffalo on September 14, but too

President McKinley is shot!

late. William McKinley had died at 2:15 a.m. Theodore borrowed a black suit and took his oath of office at 3:00 that afternoon.

"And now look," old Mark Hanna grumbled, "that damned cowboy is President of the United States!"

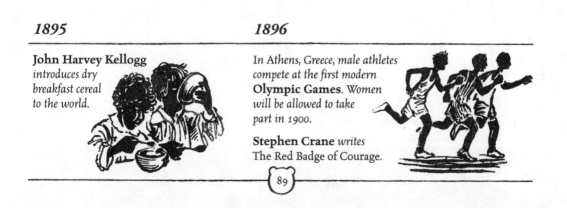

1895

John Harvey Kellogg *introduces dry breakfast cereal to the world.*

1896

In Athens, Greece, male athletes compete at the first modern **Olympic Games**. *Women will be allowed to take part in 1900.*

Stephen Crane *writes* The Red Badge of Courage.

Lively times in the White House

CHAPTER FOUR

Roosevelts in the White House 1901–1909

A BLAST OF FRESH AIR

THE NATION MOURNED. On his first day in the White House, September 23, 1901, Theodore invited his sisters to dinner. It was, they remembered, their father's 70th birthday. To Theodore, it was as if Thee's hand was on his shoulder, giving him his blessing. A somber day all right, and it was awful that he was President on account of an assassin's bullet, but Theodore refused to dwell on that. He'd do his best to do the big job right. In fact, he relished the opportunity.

Americans had never had such a young President, and

1896

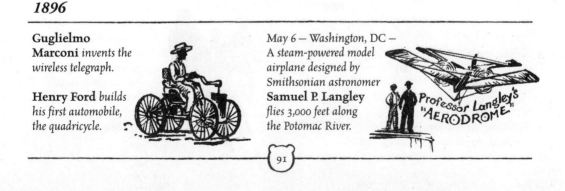

Guglielmo Marconi *invents the wireless telegraph.*

Henry Ford *builds his first automobile, the quadricycle.*

May 6 — Washington, DC — A steam-powered model airplane designed by Smithsonian astronomer **Samuel P. Langley** *flies 3,000 feet along the Potomac River.*

Professor Langley's "AERODROME"

never one like Theodore, a most serious, well-read man who also practiced boxing in the White House. At least he did until a punch from one of his sparring partners left him blind in one eye.

One day in Washington, he was seen making faces while riding in his carriage. Was he nutty? No, up the street were Archie and Quentin in a trolley, grimacing at their dad, who responded with equally monstrous expressions. "You must remember," said an old friend, "the president is about six." No President ever led diplomats on adventurous nature hikes like Theodore did. Once, when he stripped to his shorts in order to swim across a creek, the French ambassador had to do the same. He left his lavender gloves on though, "in case," the Frenchman explained, "we meet ladies."

Americans were totally fascinated with the Roosevelt kids, especially 4-year-old Quentin and beautiful, bratty Alice, 17. Ted was 14; Kermit, 12; Ethel, 10; and Archie was 7. It wasn't easy for them all to fit into the 100-year-old mansion, along with the President's offices and the visiting public. Still, its old halls were great for roller-skating and stilt walking. Alice and her siblings slid down the stairs on big tin trays from the pantry and played with their many pets, such as Alice's green snake, Emily Spinach; Quentin's pink-eyed rabbits; Eli the big blue macaw; Allan the

1896

Aug. 17 —
A discovery in Canada's Yukon Territory will spark next year's Klondike gold rush.

Nov. 3 —
William McKinley *is elected 25th U.S. President.*

1897

Bram Stoker *writes* Dracula.

After a dozen years of subduing the people of Madagascar, French colonists take over the island and end the reign of **Queen Ranavalona.**

The Roosevelt kids

terrier; and Archie's badger, Josiah. Once, Quentin coaxed their Shetland pony, Algonquin, into the elevator to visit Archie, who was sick upstairs. All sorts of dogs and cats came to live at the White House as well as kangaroo rats, a flying squirrel, Bill the lizard, guinea pigs, and a particular kitten, known for grabbing the ankle of old Mr. Cannon, Speaker of the House.

1897

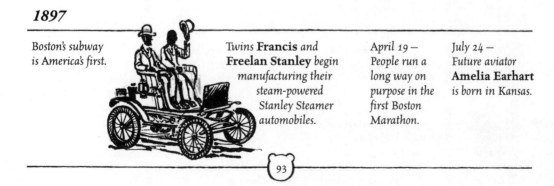

Boston's subway is America's first.

Twins **Francis** and **Freelan Stanley** begin manufacturing their steam-powered Stanley Steamer automobiles.

April 19 — People run a long way on purpose in the first Boston Marathon.

July 24 — Future aviator **Amelia Earhart** is born in Kansas.

MR. PRESIDENT

THEODORE PROMISED TO MIND THE STORE just as McKinley had done, but conservative business leaders were wary of their young, unpredictable President. They'd likely frown at his proclaiming forest and wildlife reserves all over the place (see page 106). Anyway, his first big controversy wasn't at all about the economy or conservation. It had to do with dinner.

When Theodore invited one of the most influential educators of his time to dine with him, he made thousands of citizens furious and gave others a sliver of hope. How so? His guest was Booker T. Washington, the first African American ever invited to dinner at the White House. Theodore, not wanting to dim his chance of winning the 1904 election, did it only once. As he well knew, America had a wide racist streak.

This was a time when companies were combining into big

1898   **1899**

Dowager Empress Cixi (*a.k.a.* **Tz'u-Hsi** *or* **Xiao Qin Xian**), *seizes control of China.*

Valdemar Poulsen *of Denmark invents his telegraphone, the first machine that records sound magnetically.*

H. G. Wells, *author of* The Time Machine (1895) *and* The Invisible Man (1897) *writes* War of the Worlds.

Bicycling is all the fashion in the 1890s. Horse-drawn vehicles share the road with millions of men, boys, women, and girls on bikes.

monopolies known as "combines" or "trusts." In 1901, three men, including the fabulously powerful banker J. P. Morgan, formed the National Securities Company (NSC). It would control one fourth of the country's railroads, the main way goods and people traveled. Theodore wasn't alone in thinking that such a big, fat trust would squash competition and lead to high prices. He really shook up the business world when he said that the NSC was against the law – the Sherman Anti-Trust Act, to be exact. Morgan himself went to talk to him, but Theodore was politely determined that men whose only power was money should not be bigger than the U.S. government. Its power was from the people.

"I have always been fond of the West African proverb," Theodore said. "Speak softly and carry a big stick, you will go far."

Dinner with Mr. Washington

1899

American dancer **Isadora Duncan** *begins performing in Europe. Her very individual, flowing sort of movement and dress revolutionize the art of dance.*

Pianist and composer **Scott Joplin** *specializes in a new, exciting kind of music: ragtime.*

Oct 12 – Three years of Boer War begins as Dutch and British settlers in southernmost Africa begin fighting.

Other businesses trying to control the nation's copper, electricity, and such found themselves in the way of his administration's big stick. Folks called Theodore the "trustbuster," but really, he didn't want big corporations busted, just *regulated* (given some rules to go by). As it turned out, the Supreme Court ruled in 1904 that the NSC was, indeed, illegal.

A far worse crisis flared up in May 1902 when 140,000 Pennsylvania coal miners went on strike, desperate for a raise. They worked long hard hours down in the dark for an average annual salary of $400. There was no compensation, either, if they were hurt or killed, which happened often. But the owners, who considered it their God-given right to control the mines as they saw fit, refused to talk to John Mitchell, the miners' representative. Folks ran out of coal for their furnaces and engines. Winter was coming, but the strike kept on. People panicked. The President stepped in.

Theodore had Mitchell and George F. Baer, the owners' representative, come to his office, but Baer would not bend. The strike ended only when TR threatened to have the army take over the mines, and he got J. P. Morgan, the bigshot banker, to put the squeeze on the bullheaded owners. Never before had a

1899

1900

Jan. 23 — **Emilio Aguinaldo,** *who had revolted against Spanish rule over the Philippine Islands, leads those who are against U.S. occupation. A truly nasty guerrilla war breaks out between the Filipinos and the Americans (see 1901).*

U.S. population is 76,212,168. The world population is up to 1.65 billion.

L. Frank Baum *writes* The Wonderful Wizard of Oz.

President gotten in the middle of a strike like that, much less settled it in favor of the workers, who got a 10 percent raise in pay. Theodore hated violent strikes, but just as bad, in his eyes, were greedy bosses who provoked workers with their arrogant ways.

Meanwhile, as workmen were fixing and expanding the White House, Theodore had a brush with death one bright September day in Massachusetts. A trolley car crashed into his carriage, killed a Secret Service man and a horse, and catapulted TR through the air. His bruises faded, but his hurt leg would always bother him. Still, two months later, he managed to go bear hunting down in Mississippi. No way would Theodore shoot the one bear he saw. She'd been caught for him and tied to a tree! Cartoons showing this presidential pardon inspired a New York toymaker to sew the first "teddy" bear.

In December 1902, Theodore felt well enough to defend the Western Hemisphere, threatening force (that "big stick" again) if German ships didn't leave the waters off Venezuela. (It owed Germany lots of money it had borrowed.)

Teddy Bear

1900

Thousands of amateur photographers will be taking millions of pictures with their new $1 Brownie box cameras made by **George Eastman**'s Kodak company.

Escape artist **Ehrich Weiss**, a.k.a. **Harry Houdini**, begins his remarkable career this year.

Max Planck, *quantum physics pioneer, proposes the revolutionary idea that shining light is made of the smallest possible bits of energy: quanta.*

It was built in 1792-1800, totally repaired after the 1814 fire. The North Portico was added in 1829.

WHITE HOUSE

West Terrace

East Terrace

East Wing

West Wing
The Oval Office
was added
in 1909.

South Portico, added 1824.

Gutted, rebuilt 1949. 1942. Gutted, rebuilt 1949. shelter, map room, movie theater:

The mansion got gaslight in 1848, a telephone in 1877, and in 1891, electricity. What else? A new 3rd floor: 1927. Indoor swimming pool: 1933. Bomb

THIS OLD HOUSE

When a well-dressed crowd came to one of the many presidential events, the floors had to be propped up with timbers or Theodore and his guests might wind up in the dingy cellar! It'd be the job of architect Charles McKim to make the crowded old President's House useful, beautiful, and strong. In summer 1902, Congress came up with $475,445 to pay for the job. By Christmas, new rooms, refurbished and reorganized, graced the basement, attic, and the two floors in between. The presidential offices were moved to the new building west of the old mansion, known now by its new official name: the White House.

1900

English archaeologist **Arthur Evans** begins excavating the ancient palace at Knossos on the island of Crete.

In China, secret societies of peasants attack and kill Westerners and Chinese Christians. U.S. troops join rescuers from other nations to crush this "Boxer Rebellion."

June 14 — Hawaii officially becomes a U.S. territory.

THE CANAL IN PANAMA

FOR CENTURIES, ANY MARINER BOLD ENOUGH TO SAIL to or from the Atlantic to the Pacific Ocean had to go thousands of extra miles around South America. Sailors grumbled, engineers pondered, and dreamers dreamed of a way to do what any mapmaker could do with a stroke of a pen: Cut through the skinny isthmus between the Americas. The way he did it angered more than a few people, but TR made the grand shortcut possible.

Many thought higher, dryer Nicaragua would be the best place. Many others preferred Colombia's narrow province of Panama. In the 1850s, thousands toiled through Panama's jungles to shorten their trips to the California goldfields. In the 1880s, a French attempt to build a canal in Panama was doomed by poor tools, fevers, and shifty dealing. In 1902, the U.S. stepped in, but Colombia's sudden demand for lots more money made Theodore

1900

Sept. 8 — More than 6,000 people die when a huge hurricane pounds Galveston, Texas.

1901

In the Philippines, U.S. troops capture **Emilio Aguinaldo** and set up a government headed by **William Howard Taft**.

furious. He basically looked the other way when Panamanians revolted, ending their strained relationship with the Colombian government. That freed the U.S., in 1903, to make a treaty with independent Panama and pay it $10 million plus $250,000 annual rent (as of 1913) for the use and control of a canal zone.

Disease, not land, was the biggest obstacle. Theodore himself still had attacks of his "Cuban fever." In Cuba, in 1900, Army doctor Walter Reed learned how to fight typhoid and yellow fevers by killing the flies and mosquitoes that spread these diseases. With that knowledge, work in the tropics was made possible. From 1904 to 1914, at a cost of $380 million, thousands of workers accomplished one of the world's great feats of engineering. In 1906, Theodore and Edith would go see the canal being built, becoming the first President and First Lady to travel to a foreign country while in office.

The Western Hemisphere's awesome shortcut

1901

Jan. 10 —
It's a gusher! An awful lot of oil is discovered at Spindletop, near Beaumont, Texas. Oil drilling begins in Persia (present-day Iran) this year, but drillers won't hit it big until 1908.

Jan. 22 —
Queen Victoria *dies at 81. Now her 59-year-old son will be* **King Edward VII**. *That's why people call these next few years Edwardian.*

1902

Beatrix Potter *writes and illustrates* The Tale of Peter Rabbit.

THE BIG PARADE

THEODORE WAS IN OFFICE because of the death of William McKinley. This sad fact made TR determined to win the next presidential race, but he knew that no election was a sure thing. "Even if I am beaten," he wrote to Kermit, "you must remember that we have had three years of great enjoyment out of the Presidency and that we are mighty lucky to have had them."

On November 8, Democrat Alton B. Parker was buried under Theodore's landslide of 1904. That night, however, the President seemed to have the 1908 election on his mind. "Under no circumstances," read the statement he issued, "will I be a candidate for or accept another nomination." Bullheaded Theodore would wish again and again that he could take his words back, but no. That would be against his code of honor.

Old Secretary of State John Hay had been President Lincoln's

1902

Arthur Conan Doyle *writes* The Hound of the Baskervilles.

New York City gets one of its first skyscrapers: the triangular, 21-story Flatiron Building.

This year, 16-year-old **Alphonso XIII** *begins his reign as king of Spain, and U.S. troops pull out of independent Cuba.*

secretary and had known Thee. Now Hay gave Theodore a ring with a lock of Lincoln's hair tucked inside to wear on his Inauguration Day, March 4, 1905. How Theodore wished that his father could be there to witness the oath of office, the brass bands, and Rough Riders galloping through the triumphant parade.

In his second term, TR worked to control the rates railroads charged. After he read *The Jungle*, Upton Sinclair's 1906 bombshell-bestseller about the meatpacking industry, Theodore ordered a Congressional investigation. Big laws were passed to make sure meat, other foods, and drugs didn't make people sick. This time in America was known for muckraking writers such as Mr. Sinclair, Ida M. Tarbell, and Lincoln Steffens. "Muckraker" was TR's term for those who investigated and dug through the dirty, mean, greedy parts of modern life.

When France and Germany were bickering over Morocco, Theodore helped to prevent a war. Demonstrating truly slick diplomatic skills, he helped to end a war between Japan and Russia. In doing so, Theodore became the first American to win a Nobel Prize for Peace in 1906. On the other hand, as he liked to say, there was the Texas incident.

A white man was killed in Brownsville that summer of 1906.

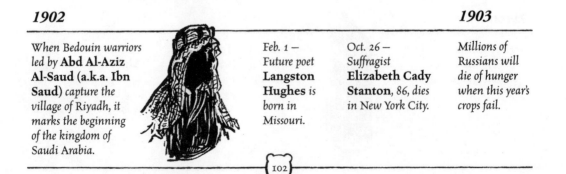

1902

When Bedouin warriors led by **Abd Al-Aziz Al-Saud (a.k.a. Ibn Saud)** *capture the village of Riyadh, it marks the beginning of the kingdom of Saudi Arabia.*

Feb. 1 — Future poet **Langston Hughes** *is born in Missouri.*

Oct. 26 — Suffragist **Elizabeth Cady Stanton**, *86, dies in New York City.*

1903

Millions of Russians will die of hunger when this year's crops fail.

African-American soldiers, who'd recently been stationed nearby, were blamed, though no one was named or charged. Theodore agreed that the soldiers must know who was guilty, so he discharged all 167 men in the regiment, without honor. Six had won Medals of Honor (the prize Theodore really wanted) in Cuba and in the Philippines. Probably just as well Thee wasn't alive to see how unfair his son was in this instance (see page 132).

WHITE HOUSE WEDDING
AND THE GREAT WHITE FLEET

WHEN SHE WAS TINY, HER FATHER LEFT HER and could barely speak her name. Now "Alice" was in hit songs, given to new babies, and ladies wore "Alice Blue" gowns, the color of her steely eyes. "Father doesn't care for me," she told her diary, "one eighth as much as he does for the other children." She both loved and

1903

Jack London *writes* The Call of the Wild.

Both the Harley-Davidson motorcycle and the Tour de France bicycle race are introduced this year.

Helen Keller, *18, blind and deaf since she was a baby, writes* The Story of My Life.

TR, Edith, beautiful, troublesome Alice, and her snake, Emily Spinach

resented him. If her rebellious flirting, smoking, and racetrack gambling didn't get the attention she wanted from her father, they surely horrified ladylike Edith. Couldn't Theodore control her, a friend asked?

On February 17, 1906, crowds converged on the White House, all hoping to see Alice in her satin-and-lace wedding gown or at least Congressman Nick Longworth, her bald-headed groom. Less than a year before, Theodore stole the show at Franklin and Eleanor Roosevelt's wedding. As Alice would say, "My father always wanted to be the corpse at every funeral, the bride at every wedding and the baby at every christening."

1903

Edwin S. Porter *makes one of the very first movies to tell a story:* The Great Train Robbery *(running time: 11 min.) People pay 5¢ to see it in nickelodeons, the first movie theaters.*

May 23 – July 26 —
Dr. Horatio Nelson Jackson, Sewell Crocker, *and* **Bud** *the dog travel across mostly unpaved America in a Winton automobile in the nation's first cross-country car trip.*

As young Teedie, TR had idolized his uncles in the Confederate Navy. His first book was about war at sea. Then there was his lively year at the Navy Department. On March 25, 1905, he became the first President to dive down in a submarine, the USS *Plunger*. And on December 16, 1907, he sent 16 gleaming white battleships, the "Great White Fleet," away on a goodwill voyage to show off America's naval power to the world.

The Great White Fleet

TR invited the nation's governors, scientists, environmental experts, and the Supreme Court justices to a White House conservation conference in 1908. They set up a commission to inventory the nation's natural resources, something that had never been done before. Later on, he would invite men from the U.S., Canada, and Mexico to confer about North America's environment.

1903

Marie Sklodowska Curie *becomes the first woman to win a Nobel Prize in Physics for her study of radioactivity. In 1911, she'll win the Nobel Prize in Chemistry.*

Dec. 17 – Kitty Hawk, NC– **Orville** *and* **Wilbur Wright** *of Dayton, OH, accomplish the first successful flight of a heavier-than-air machine.*

CONSERVE AND PROTECT

The boy who loved nature became a man who used his powers to protect it so it could go on being loved. In 1888, TR started the Boone and Crockett Club to protect animal habitats, the first club of its kind. It inspired similar organizations such as the Sierra Club, founded in 1892 by John Muir, and helped to bring about 1894's Park Protection Act. It gave the government the power to save Yellowstone National Park and the animals that lived there from being destroyed by ruthless builders and promoters.

As President, TR set up a National Conservation Congress (1908), inspiring 41 states to begin their own environmental programs. On behalf of the American people, he added 150 million acres of woodland to U.S. land reserves, and, in 1905, he began the U.S. Forest Service. He established 18 national monuments including Niagara Falls. He doubled America's national parks when he added Colorado's Mesa Verde and four others to the list. He set aside 51 wildlife preserves, the first being Florida's Pelican Islands. Too many of its birds had given their lives for ladies' plumed hats. TR used his job's "bully pulpit" — meaning that when the President talks, people listen — to make Americans aware of their duty "to protect ourselves and our children against the wasteful development of our natural resources."

1904

Japan attacks Russian ships at Port Arthur in southern Manchuria. Meanwhile, Russians are finishing work on the world's longest train track: the Trans-Siberian Railroad. It stretches nearly 3,200 miles from Moscow to Vladivostok.

People at the Louisiana Purchase Exposition in St. Louis, MO, have their first tastes of iced tea, hamburgers, and ice-cream cones. And, at this world's fair, America gets its first Olympic Games.

Theodore got a bang out of being President. Now, in between his regular duties, he was planning the next chapter of his life. He gave the White House Gang (ten-year-old Quentin, his friend Charlie Taft, and their buddies) a stern talking to for sticking spitballs on the presidential portraits, and he chose Charlie's dad to be the Republican's next presidential candidate. Tubby, sweet-smiling William Howard Taft had been the Secretary of War, the Governor of the Philippines, and Theodore's good friend. As it happened, Democrat William Jennings Bryan, who'd lost in 1896 and 1900, lost again in 1908 to big Will Taft.

Quentin, TR, Charlie, and Mr. Taft

Ten days after Theodore welcomed home the Great White Fleet on February 22, 1909, icy winds howled through Washington on Taft's Inauguration Day. Theodore's Presidency was over, and his next adventure was about to begin. He could hardly wait.

1904

London, England —
James Barrie *debuts his play* Peter Pan or The Boy Who Would Not Grow Up.

Milan, Italy —
Giacomo Puccini *debuts his opera,* Madame Butterfly.

1905

Sarah B. Walker, *a.k.a.*
Madame C. J. Walker,
becomes the first millionaire businesswoman of color, having successfully marketed the hair preparation she developed.

The illustration border reads: PRESIDENTIAL CANDIDATE · JUNGLE EXPLORER · AUTHOR · SPEECHMAKER · DAD · GRANDFATHER · THEODORE ROOSEVELT · WORLD TRAVELER · BIG GAME HUNTER · THIRD-PARTY

TR: *Super American*

CHAPTER FIVE

The Rest of His Life
1909–1919

THE WILDS OF AFRICA

So what was a 50-year-old ex-President to do? Theodore was going hunting in Africa and would write about his experiences. Naturalists and taxidermists from the Smithsonian Institution would join the expedition to help collect wildlife specimens. Theodore took restless 19-year-old Kermit along on the safari to experience "the hardy life of the open, in long rides rifle in hand, in the thrill of the fight with dangerous game." Theodore wanted to see Africa's "silent places...the large tropic moons, and the splendor of new stars."

1905

Albert Einstein publishes his revolutionary notions about space, time, and energy and how they relate to each other.

In the rough game of football, helmets are not yet customary; 18 players die this year alone, and 154 are seriously hurt. **President Roosevelt** invites college sports administrators to the White House, convincing them to make the game less brutal.

On March 23, 1909, father and son climbed aboard an ocean liner. J. P. Morgan was said to have declared, "America expects that every lion will do his duty" [and have troublesome Teddy for dinner!] They sailed across the Atlantic Ocean, the Mediterranean Sea, through the Suez Canal to the Red Sea and on to the Indian Ocean, then down Africa's coast to the ancient seaport of Mombasa in British East Africa (present-day Kenya).

Along with his rifles, Theodore brought 37 pigskin-bound histories, novels, and such, so he'd have something to read "perhaps beside the carcass of a beast I had killed." He and Kermit and the others traveled first class, along with about 250 Swahili and Arab porters, gun bearers, soldiers, "tent boys," and *saises*, those who tended the horses.

Theodore was blind in one eye from boxing; he had a bum leg from the runaway trolley, and a big belly from too many White House dinners. Still, he and Kermit shot 17 lions, 11 elephants, 20 rhinoceroses, 9 giraffes, 47 gazelles, 8 hippopotamuses, 9 hyenas, and 29 zebras, as well as various antelopes: bongo, kudu, and dik-dik. All in all, they bagged 512 animals.

"Kermit and I kept about a dozen trophies for ourselves," Theodore wrote later on in defense of all this carnage, "otherwise

1905

Jan. 22 —
Russians are suffering hunger, labor unrest, and pogroms (organized killing of Jews). Thousands of unarmed folks wanting government reform go to the czar's Winter Palace in St. Petersburg. There they are attacked by mounted soldiers and troops with blazing machine guns.

Sept. 1 —
Two new provinces are formed in Canada: Alberta and Saskatchewan.

we shot nothing that was not used either for a museum specimen or for meat—usually for both."

In the evenings, in his tent, Theodore scratched out thousands of words as the lamp flickered, as campfire tales were told, as smoke curled up into the treetops where African birds called, and as the saises, Hamisi and Simba, picked ticks off the horses.

African evening

After the African safari and after his trip through Europe, Theodore came home on June 18, 1910, to a shrieking of steam whistles, firing of guns, and the happy roar of the biggest crowd that had ever filled the streets of New York City. A cartoon on the cover of *Harper's Weekly* showed a joyful American eagle flapping

1906

Lee De Forest's invention, the triode vacuum tube, amplifies sound and makes radio and television possible.

Citizens of Iran use their people power to force **Shah Muzaffar al-Din** *to give them a constitution and a parliament.*

*Feb. 10 —
Arms race! Great Britain's HUGE new battleship* Dreadnought *inspires German* **Kaiser (Emperor) Wilhelm II** *to build bigger warships of his own.*

Theodore and the GREAT WORLD
March 23, 1909 to June 18, 1910

Kermit

⇒ BUDAPEST ⇒ PARIS ⇒ BRUSSELS ⇒ The Hague ⇒ COPENHAGEN

ROME ⇒ VIENNA

Christiana (OSLO) where TR accepted his NOBEL Prize ⇒ BERLIN

CAIRO

NILE RIVER
EGYPT

③ Edith and Ethel met TR and Kermit at on March 14, 1910. Together the Roosevelts traveled north on the NILE to CAIRO. TR's journey took him on to the capitals of EUROPE.

KHARTOUM

WHITE NILE

BLUE NILE

② Then, until February, 1910, TR, Kermit, and the other hunters, native soldiers, and more than 250 porters tracked and killed game in the CONGO.

AFRICA

SOMALI LAND

Abyssinia

Italian territory

Theodore's safari hunted in British East Africa, now known as KENYA.

EQUATOR

INDIAN OCEAN

① KERMIT and TR arrive at MOMBASA April 21, 1909

(MASAILAND)

Lake Victoria Nyanza

Mount Kilimanjaro

USA ⇐ Gibraltar ⇐ Naples ⇐ Khartoum ⇐ Mombasa ⇐

⇐ home

LONDON (TR represented the U.S. at the funeral of King EDWARD VII)

1906

April 18 – 5:13 a.m.. — Between San Francisco's terrible earthquake and the equally terrible fire that followed, nearly 2,500 people die. Many more lose their homes.

June 25 — New York City — Brilliant, famous architect **Stanford White**, who once fancied the beautiful actress/model **Evelyn Nesbitt**, is murdered by Evelyn's husband, eccentric millionaire **Harry K. Thaw**, at Madison Square Garden (designed by White). Americans go into a total tabloid tizzy over the sensational murder trial.

his wings as a teddy bear danced and a small Theodore jumped into the arms of Uncle Sam who says, "My boy."

BULL MOOSE

IN WASHINGTON, there were those who found President Taft a lot easier to work with than his forceful predecessor. As a result, many of Theodore's policies were falling by the wayside, to TR's dismay. Again and again he'd said he was done with politics, but when folks kept bringing up a possible run in 1912, Theodore could not resist a chance to win his old job back. "My hat is in the ring!" he exclaimed, inventing a new expression. It meant that he was in the fight.

Around the country, before seas of people topped with feathered hats, derbies, and fedoras, he delivered thumping speeches, delighting the crowds. He waved at them from high

1907

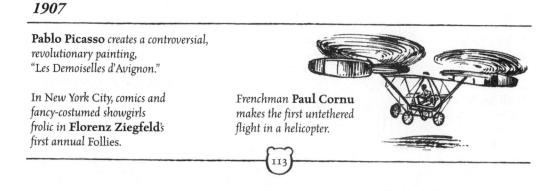

Pablo Picasso *creates a controversial, revolutionary painting, "Les Demoiselles d'Avignon."*

In New York City, comics and fancy-costumed showgirls frolic in **Florenz Ziegfeld's** *first annual* Follies.

Frenchman **Paul Cornu** *makes the first untethered flight in a helicopter.*

aloft in an airplane – the first for him or for any President. In Chicago, at the Republicans' national convention, a huge audience paraded, stamped their feet, waved flags and banners, and clapped and hollered for "Teddy!" In the end, however, the powerful party leaders steamrollered Will Taft to the nomination.

Nearly two months later, Theodore was still furious when he became the leader of the Progressive Party. Now, it wasn't long before this third political party, made up of angry, breakaway Republicans and old Populists, became known as the Bull Moose Party. Why? Because once when someone asked TR about his health, Theodore promptly replied that he was "as fit as a bull moose!" That was good because it would take a superman to get all that the Progressives were wanting: an 8-hour workday, women's right to vote, and the end of child labor, among other radical things. This was pretty hot stuff and rather ahead of America's time, but the Progressives were certain that Teddy was the man to make these dreams come true.

As in nearly all campaigns, harsh things were said.

TR, Taft, and their opponent New Jersey Governor Woodrow Wilson were no exception. At the end of one long day, a reporter found worn-out Will Taft sitting alone.

1907

Robert Baden-Powell *of Great Britain starts the Boy Scouts.* William Boyce *will begin the American Boy Scouts in 1910.*

July 6 —
Future artist Frida Kahlo *is born in Mexico.*

Nov. 16 —
Oklahoma becomes the 46th state.

1908

Kenneth Grahame *writes* The Wind in the Willows.

Lucy Maud Montgomery *writes* Anne of Green Gables.

"Roosevelt was my closest friend," he said, and began to weep.

As summer turned to fall and election day neared, Theodore had enough political savvy to sense that the Democratic candidate was going to win the race. Woodrow Wilson, former president of Princeton University, looked like a stern schoolmaster, but he was a fine speechmaker with a strong progressive reputation of his own. Theodore kept hard at the campaigning, of course. He refused to give up – not even after a would-be assassin tried to kill him! John Schrank claimed that William McKinley, in a dream, had inspired him to take a shot at TR. It happened in Milwaukee, Wisconsin. Theodore ordered the outraged onlookers not to hurt "the poor creature," then, before he'd go to a hospital, he insisted on speaking to his waiting audience.

"Friends," he said, "I am going to ask you to be very quiet. . . . I'll do the best I can, but there is a bullet in my body." He unbuttoned his vest, dramatically revealing his bloody shirt. He held up 50 folded pages worth of bullet-ripped speech.

"No!" The people gasped. "Oh no!"

Theodore reassured them. It would take more than a bullet "to kill a Bull Moose!" On and on he talked, voice faltering, face pale.

"No man has had a happier life than I have. . . ."

1908

Former Civil War scout **Harriet Tubman,** who led many a slave to freedom, opens a home in Auburn, NY, for poor and elderly black folks.

Aug. 12 — **Henry Ford** introduces his Model T automobile.

Aug. 27 — **Lyndon Baines Johnson,** future President, is born in Texas.

Nov. 3 — **William Howard Taft** is elected. He'll be the 27th U.S. President.

An A-1 time for the old Bull Moose

"No, Sir!" Theodore snapped when a friend tried to quiet him. "You can't stop me nor anybody else." Then, to the crowd he said, "I have had an A-1 time in life and I'm having it now!"

Indeed he was. He spoke to that crowd for an hour and a half. His coat, his folded speech, and dense chest muscles kept the bullet out of his lung. As for the election of 1912, Taft came in third, TR second, and Woodrow Wilson won the Presidency.

1909

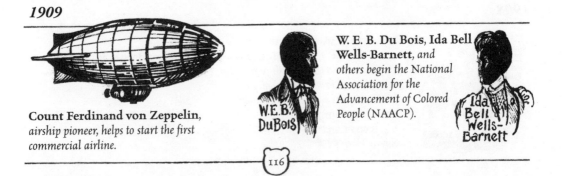

Count Ferdinand von Zeppelin, *airship pioneer, helps to start the first commercial airline.*

W. E. B. Du Bois, Ida Bell Wells-Barnett, *and others begin the National Association for the Advancement of Colored People* (NAACP).

THE RIVER OF DOUBT

THE DEFEAT HURT THEODORE far more than the assassin's bullet and took a lot longer to heal – if it ever did. He busied himself with writing his autobiography and attending Ethel's wedding. And TR sued a Michigan newspaperman for writing that he was a liar and a drunk. (The editor had to apologize and pay Theodore 6 cents.) Afterwards, in the fall of 1913, Theodore went adventuring. It was his last chance to be a boy, so he said, and it nearly killed him.

Once again, Theodore and Kermit traveled together, this time over the peaks of the Andes then through the Brazilian jungle to join an expedition to map the *Río da Divuda*, River of Doubt, a most appropriate name.

It was as if the fire ants and mosquitoes were defending the jungle from trespassers. On February 6, 1914, 22 men in 7 wooden dugout canoes set off down the wild river. It was horrible;

1909

April 6 –
Robert E. Peary *and Matthew Henson of America are the first to reach the North Pole.*

1910

President Taft *throws out the first ball of the season and starts a big league baseball tradition.*

After a successful rebellion against **Porfirio Diaz's** *dictatorship, things are mighty unsettled as men such as* **Francisco "Pancho" Villa** *and* **Emiliano Zapata** *struggle for control of Mexico (see March 9, 1916).*

Theodore and the River of Doubt

5 canoes and 3 men were lost – one by murder. Theodore's bad leg was banged up in the rapids and infected in no time. Sick, helpless, he begged Kermit to leave him behind so he wouldn't have to carry him. Delirious with fever, he mumbled poetry. At last, on April 30, the explorers emerged from the jungle, having mapped

1910

1911

Japan annexes Korea.

The Union of South Africa is established.

May 6 –
King Edward VII is dead. Long live **George V** of Great Britain, cousin of both **Nicholas**, czar of Russia, and Germany's **Emperor Wilhelm**. George's granddaughter is present-day **Queen Elizabeth II**.

King GEORGE V

"Alexander's Ragtime Band," by **Irving Berlin**, is a monster hit song, and plenty of people are doing the Turkey Trot made popular by celebrity dancing duo **Vernon** and **Irene Castle**.

the 1,000-mile river, known these days as the Rio Roosevelt or sometimes, Rio Teodoro. Thin, tired Theodore managed a joke when he returned to New York. "You see," giving his cane a wave, "I still have the big stick!"

He was able to go to Spain in June, when heroic Kermit married the daughter of America's ambassador there. It was later that month, in the city of Sarajevo, that a Serbian student shot a pair of Austrian royals. Who could imagine that this would spark all-out war? This was the 20th century. Civilization had progressed beyond barbaric warfare, hadn't it?

The survivor

1911

Feb. 6 —
Ronald Reagan, *future President, is born in Illinois.*

Mar. 25 —
Fire in New York City's Triangle Shirtwaist Factory kills 146 people, mostly young women, in smoke, flames, or desperate jumps.

Aug. 6 —
Lucille Ball, *future actress, television star, and business-woman, is born in New York.*

THE GREAT ADVENTURE

~M~

AUSTRIA REACTED TO THE MURDERS BY DECLARING WAR on Serbia. This set off a chain reaction from Vienna to Moscow. Europe's jealous, competitive rulers had formed *alliances* (promises to join their allies' battles), so off went their armies to war.

When Germany trampled over Belgium and its navy sank neutral vessels, Americans were outraged but determined to stay out of the fight. To Theodore, it was feeble not to choose sides when faced with right and wrong. The U.S. must be made ready for war! It had hurt him to watch Taft handle the reins of power, but seeing Wilson in the saddle was *agony*. Theodore knew that a leader's chance to show true historical greatness came only in times of crisis. Now the deepest crisis of the age was flaming across Europe, and Theodore's Presidency was over. He seethed with frustration.

1911   **1912**

Dec. 14 —
Norwegian **Roald Amundsen** *is the first to reach the South Pole. English-man* **Robert F. Scott** *and four other explorers get there a few weeks later but die of cold and hunger on the return trek.*

Hans Geiger *invents the Geiger counter. People use it to detect radioactive elements.*

Maria Montessori *publishes her methods of teaching young children to read.*

On May 7, 1915, a German torpedo struck the *Lusitania*, a British ship, and killed 1,198 passengers, including 128 Americans. Innocent people were lost because of "Wilson's abject cowardice and weakness," Theodore raged in a letter to Kermit.

As hundreds of thousands of soldiers were dying in Europe, young men in the U.S., including Theodore's sons, were undergoing military training in privately funded "preparedness camps." In hot letters and speeches, Theodore campaigned for his two passions: preparedness and "real Americanism." How, he demanded, could people who called themselves German-Americans or English-Americans ever be fully united, patriotic, loyal, and prepared for war? Instead of "hyphenated Americans," everyone must be "Americans through and through!"

Theodore would've campaigned for President too, but the Progressives were too dispirited and the Republicans were too mad at him for splitting the party in 1912. Would he have won if he'd run in 1916? Many still flocked to see and hear Teddy, that's for sure. Many others grew tired of his ranting about war.

Wilson was reelected, and what was his campaign slogan? "He Kept Us Out of War." And so he did, until Germany said it might well attack U.S. ships. After all, they could be helping its

1912

Jan. 1 —
Leaders of a long revolt against China's Manchu rulers establish the Republic of China. **Sun Yat-sen** *is its temporary president.*

Feb. 12 —
After 267 years, the Manchu dynasty falls. China's last emperor, 6-year-old **Puyi,** *no longer has the power to rule.*

Mar. 12 —
Juliette Gordon "Daisy" Low *of Savannah, GA, starts the American Girl Scouts.*

enemies, Britain and France. What's more, the Germans promised the return of lost Mexican lands – California, Texas, and the American Southwest – if Mexico would help by invading the U.S.A.

As of April 6, 1917, the U.S. was in the fight.

America really had to scramble. It wasn't ready. Hadn't Teddy been saying so? Suddenly, he was more popular than ever to folks frenzied with patriotic war fever. Movie stars went all over the place, encouraging citizens to buy "Liberty" bonds and cut back on gas, meat, and flour. No sacrifice was too great for the war effort! Sheep nibbled on the White House lawn. Their wool went into uniforms and the socks girls and boys knit for the troops.

Sheep on the White House lawn

Americans went a bit nuts. German music and language classes were cancelled or banned. Folks were cruel to those with German-sounding names. Little dachshunds, "wiener dogs," were

1912   **1913**

April 14 – 15 –
*The British ocean liner
Titanic collides with an
iceberg!. Nearly 1,500
passengers die when the
great ship goes down to
the bottom of the
Atlantic Ocean.*

April 16 –
*American journalist/
aviator* **Harriet
Quimby** *becomes
the first woman to
fly a plane across the
English Channel.*

Jan. 9 –
Richard Nixon,
*future President, is
born in California.*

known to be kicked off sidewalks. If you criticized the war, you could be arrested for aiding the enemy.

For his part, Theodore was like a lame, half-blind lion, straining at his chains for one last battle. To cast and star in a Rough Riders sequel was his chief desire, and the only one who could make it happen was the man he'd been attacking for months. So imagine the 59-year-old Colonel paying a call on "that lily-

The Colonel and the President

livered skunk" in the White House. You'll be happy to know that it was a polite visit, but Woodrow Wilson knew that the horrendous, high-tech warfare in Europe was entirely different from the 1898 Cuba campaign. He refused Theodore's request. There would be no second act. Theodore never forgave him.

1913   1914

| Feb. 4 — **Rosa Lee Parks**, *future civil rights reformer, is born in Alabama.* | July 14 — **Leslie King**, a.k.a. **Gerald Ford**, *future President, is born in Nebraska.* | **Charlie Chaplin** *becomes a world-famous film star.* | **W. C. Handy** *composes "St. Louis Blues."* |

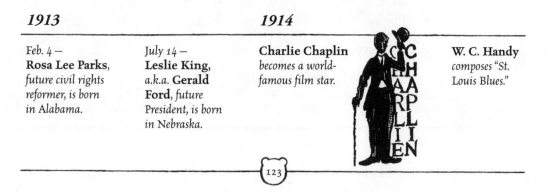

In the border (clockwise from top):

OTTOMAN EMPIRE, and BULGARIA) fought more than twenty ALLIED nations

In the First World War, Germany and the other Central Powers (Austria-Hungary, the

American poet/soldier Alan Seeger. He and about 9 million other men died in WWI.

THE GREAT WAR

The world's people of 1918 suffered through a dreadful war made worse by the Russian Revolution and a deadly pandemic. Between 20 and 40 million people were killed by the so-called "Spanish influenza," which in fact had its beginnings in China. New technologies sped the Great War's battleships, submarines, tanks, cars, trucks, motorcycles, airships, and airplanes. The fighting spread to Russia, Africa, and the Middle East, but the First World War, a.k.a. WWI, is most remembered for its aerial battles, swooping "dogfights" high over hundreds of miles of muddy, nasty trenches, where men died by the thousands in a horrible nightmare landscape known as the Western Front.

MAJOR BATTLES on the WESTERN FRONT

Antwerp, 1914
YPRES Passchendaele, 1917
Neuve 1914, 1915 Messines, 1917 Liege
Chappelle, LOOS MONS 1914
1915 Cambrai 1915 1914 Namur, 1914
Somme River, 1916 BELGIUM
Montdidier LUXEM
1918 Sedan BOUR
Aisne River 1918
BELLEAU 1914
WOODS FRANCE
1918 VERDUN
Paris Marne Chateau Meuse- 1916
Versailles River Thierry ARGONNE
1914, 1918 1918 1918

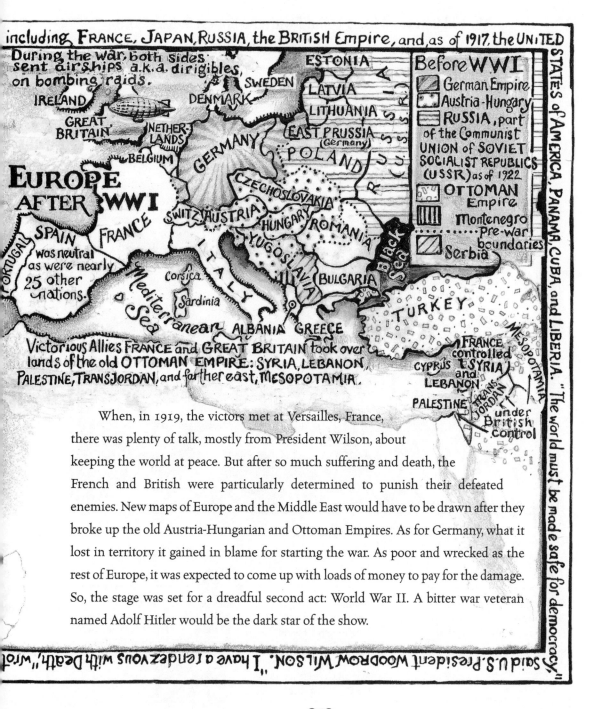

including FRANCE, JAPAN, RUSSIA, the BRITISH Empire, and, as of 1917, the UNITED

During the war, both sides sent airships a.k.a. dirigibles, on bombing raids.

IRELAND
GREAT BRITAIN
NETHER-LANDS
DENMARK
SWEDEN
ESTONIA
LATVIA
LITHUANIA
EAST PRUSSIA (Germany)
BELGIUM
GERMANY
POLAND
EUROPE AFTER WWI
SWITZ. AUSTRIA
CZECHOSLOVAKIA
HUNGARY
ROMANIA
SPAIN
FRANCE
was neutral as were nearly 25 other nations.
YUGOSLAVIA
PORTUGAL
ITALY
Corsica
Sardinia
Mediterranean Sea
BULGARIA
Black Sea
ALBANIA GREECE
TURKEY
MESOPOTAMIA

Before WWI
German Empire
Austria-Hungary
RUSSIA, part of the Communist UNION of SOVIET SOCIALIST REPUBLICS (USSR) as of 1922
OTTOMAN Empire
Montenegro
Pre-war boundaries
Serbia

STATES of AMERICA, PANAMA, CUBA, and LIBERIA. "The world must be made safe for democracy,"

Victorious Allies FRANCE and GREAT BRITAIN took over lands of the old OTTOMAN EMPIRE: SYRIA, LEBANON, PALESTINE, TRANSJORDAN, and farther east, MESOPOTAMIA.

FRANCE controlled SYRIA and LEBANON
CYPRUS
PALESTINE
TRANS-JORDAN
under British control

When, in 1919, the victors met at Versailles, France, there was plenty of talk, mostly from President Wilson, about keeping the world at peace. But after so much suffering and death, the French and British were particularly determined to punish their defeated enemies. New maps of Europe and the Middle East would have to be drawn after they broke up the old Austria-Hungarian and Ottoman Empires. As for Germany, what it lost in territory it gained in blame for starting the war. As poor and wrecked as the rest of Europe, it was expected to come up with loads of money to pay for the damage. So, the stage was set for a dreadful second act: World War II. A bitter war veteran named Adolf Hitler would be the dark star of the show.

said U.S. President Woodrow Wilson. "I have a rendezvous with Death," wrote

The old lion would stay behind with the lioness of Sagamore Hill and worry about their cubs. Alice was in Washington, and Ethel and her doctor-husband were working in a French field hospital. Fighting in France, Ted and Archie were shot, shattered, and gassed. Kermit battled Turks in Baghdad and elsewhere in Mesopotamia (now Iraq) with the British Army before joining his brothers on the Western Front. All three were decorated for gallantry.

Three of Theodore and Edith's valiant "cubs"

1914

Edgar Rice Burroughs *publishes* Tarzan of the Apes.

Aug. 3 — *The Panama Canal opens to ship traffic.*

Aug. 4 — *Germany tramples Belgium on its way to invade France. Great Britain declares war on Germany, and the Great War begins.*

Aug. 6 — *Illness takes the life of First Lady* **Ellen Wilson.**

Meanwhile, infections left over from his miserable river adventure landed Theodore in the hospital, deathly sick. He was home though, when he got word about the baby of the family.

Quentin the aviator, 20 years old, was shot and killed high in the sky over France on July 14, 1918.

"Poor Quinikins," Theodore said softly. "Poor Quinikins."

In a letter to his sister Corinne a couple of weeks later, TR wrote, "When the young die at the crest of life, in their golden morning...there is nothing more foolish and cowardly than to be beaten down by sorrow which nothing we can do will change."

It was a lesson life had taught him early on.

The eleventh hour, the eleventh day of the eleventh month – 11 a.m., November 11, 1918 – that's when the guns fell silent, and the fighting ended at last. The filthy, ruinous, agonizing, stupid, and wasteful war was over. Across the Atlantic, Theodore was in the hospital again, then back home in January, as Wilson, his old adversary, sailed off to the peace talks in France.

Up to the last, even though he was having trouble breathing, Theodore was working, writing letters, newspaper columns, and magazine articles. In the dark before dawn, January 6, 1919, a blockage in his veins quietly killed him in his bed.

1914

Oct. 21 – Nov. 22 –
Many thought that World War I would end by winter. Now, after tens of thousands of soldiers die in Belgium in the 1st Battle of Ypres, pronounced "wipers" by the Tommies (British troops), it's clear that the Great War will be horrific and last a long, long time.

1915

Movie pioneer **D. W. Griffith** *makes* Birth of a Nation. *Some scenes are very racist—and just when the Ku Klux Klan, officially shut down since the 1870s, is openly reorganizing. Its white-robed members go after "un-American" immigrants, blacks, Jews, and Roman Catholics.*

Archie, home recovering from his war wounds, telegraphed a message to his brothers: "THE OLD LION IS DEAD."

Thousands of citizens stood shivering outside the church in Oyster Bay. After the funeral, they followed the black-clad dignitaries to the snow-white cemetery. Little boys perched on bare branches to see the casket lowered into the ground. After

Will Taft's sad farewell

most everybody left, they saw a big man stay behind. William Howard Taft stood alone, with his head bowed, beside his old friend's grave.

The American people likely would have returned the complex dynamo of Sagamore Hill to the White House in 1920 if he'd lived. But he didn't, so we can only imagine what might have been

1915

Oct. 12 — British Red Cross nurse **Edith Cavell**, accused of helping Allied prisoners to escape, is shot by a German firing squad.

1916

No one had ever demonstrated outside the White House before. Now **Alice Paul** and other suffragists are standing outside its fence every day, demanding women's right to vote. They're arrested, jailed, and brutally force-fed when they refuse to eat.

and remember what really was. Remember the spindly offspring of a lion of a man; the eccentric, passionate aristocrat, transformed into a tough cowboy, ambitious politician, naturalist, and author. Remember the joyous family man, the soldier who gloried in battle, the peacemaker and statesman who did his level best to unite Americans in a sense of patriotic pride and purpose.

When his youngest son was killed, heartbroken Theodore wrote this tribute: "Only those are fit to live who do not fear to die; and none are fit to die who have shrunk from the joy of life and the duty of life. Both life and death are part of the same Great Adventure."

No words better describe the adventure of Theodore Roosevelt, one of the most interesting American lives ever lived. As words to live by, none finer could be written.

1916

Pancho Villa

Mar. 9 —
Pancho Villa *leads a deadly raid on a New Mexico town.* **President Wilson** *sends soldiers south to capture Villa. They never do.*

Oct. 16 —
Margaret Sanger *opens a birth control clinic in Brooklyn, NY, for which she's arrested and jailed.*

Nov. 4 —
Future network news anchor **Walter Cronkite** *is born in St. Joseph, MO.*

EPILOGUE

WHAT HAPPENED TO THOSE WHO LIVED AFTER? Edith Roosevelt lived out her long life in the big house at Oyster Bay. She was frail and dim at the end of her 87 years, when she died on September 30, 1948. Ethel Roosevelt Derby devoted her considerable energies to her family and to the Red Cross. And she worked to preserve her childhood home as a memorial to her dad and a window into a vanished way of life. It became an official National Historic Site in July, 1962. Before Ethel died, on December 10, 1977, she left an audio record. You can hear her talking about Sagamore Hill on S. D. Kirkpatrick's 1982 documentary, *My Father, the President.*

Kermit Roosevelt, a fine, published writer, prospered in the shipping business. He and Ted went on an expedition to Asia in 1929, looking for giant pandas. Later on, hard living and too

---

1917

The age of the czars will end after more than 350 years (see 1918) as the Bolshevik Revolution sweeps across Russia. Out of all of the violence, the communist Soviet Union (1922~1991) will rise.

In Chicago, the Original Dixieland Jass (spelling changed later on!) Band makes the first jazz recordings.

May 29 — **John Fitzgerald Kennedy,** *future President, is born in Massachusetts.*

much drinking broke his health. Kermit was 53 when he took his own life, up in Alaska on June 3, 1943.

Like his dad, Ted was a New York Assemblyman, Assistant Secretary of the Navy, a politician, and author. He governed Puerto Rico then the Philippines, before he fought the Nazis in WWII. Thanks to his injuries in WWI, he walked with a cane, but Brigadier General Ted Roosevelt, Jr. helped the Allies invade Europe on D-Day, June 6, 1944. "He repeatedly led groups from the beach, over the seawall and established them inland. His valor, courage, and presence in the very front of the attack and his complete unconcern at being under heavy fire inspired the troops to heights of enthusiasm and self-sacrifice." So it says on the citation that went with his Medal of Honor, the highest U.S. military award. A few weeks after he helped storm the beaches of Normandy, 56-year-old Ted died of a heart attack, July 12, 1944.

Theodore was passionate in his desire for a Medal of Honor of his own and in his belief that he deserved it for his actions in Cuba, but no. In his life, he had ruffled many a feather. Long after his death, though, TR's admirers continued to champion his cause. At last, on January 16, 2001, Bill Clinton, the 42nd President,

1918

Author/illustrator **Johnny Gruelle** *designs the doll Raggedy Ann.*

April 21 —
German flying ace "**Red Baron**" **Manfred von Richthofen** *famous for shooting down 80 other airplanes, is mortally wounded in his red, triple-winged Fokker.*

awarded the Medal of Honor to No. 26. Tweed Roosevelt accepted it on behalf of his great-grandfather, the only President ever to receive this lofty military honor.

Another wrong was righted in 1972, when the U.S. Government offered restitution and applied a bit of justice to that ugly 1906 deal in Brownsville, Texas, when 167 African-American soldiers were dishonorably booted out of the U.S. Army. In the decades since 1906, most of the old soldiers had died. Still, for the record, their discharges were made "honorable."

Archie, who'd barely survived WWI, was terribly wounded in WWII in the South Pacific, thus becoming the only U.S. soldier to be declared 100 percent disabled in two wars. In between, he was a successful businessman. Unlike his brothers, he grew old. A rather grim, severe old man he was by the time he died, October 13, 1979. America had gotten crowded, noisy, and polluted, it seemed to 85-year-old Archie. After all, he'd lived in a world in which, once upon a time, his little brother brought him a pony by way of the White House elevator.

Quentin, the youngest of the Roosevelt kids, was the first to die. The oldest was the last. Sharp-tongued Alice Roosevelt Longworth was so well-known in the nation's capital that folks

1918

May 15 —
The first regular U.S. airmail service is launched between New York and Washington, D.C.

July 16 —
Bolsheviks shoot and kill Russia's royal family: **Nicholas II**; *his wife,* **Alexandra**; *their daughters,* **Olga**, **Tatiana**, **Marie**, *and* **Anastasia**; *and son* **Alexis**.

called her "the other Washington Monument." She died on February 20, 1980, less than a week after her 96th birthday.

Woodrow Wilson wore himself out trying to make the U.S. part of a League of Nations, but it was not to be. A stroke in September 1919, left him so disabled that people thought that perhaps Mrs. Wilson was doing much of his job. He died in 1924, four years after winning the Nobel Peace Prize, four years after Americans chose a very different sort of leader: easygoing Warren G. Harding. (For the first time, lots of those voters were female, the 19th Amendment having been ratified on August 18, 1920.) And the winning campaign slogan? "Back to Normalcy."

But what was normal in such a changed and changing world? What would TR have made of jazz, the rise of Japan (he'd glimpsed it), the rise of ladies' skirts, and transcontinental flight? (*Dee-lighted!*) And what about the 20th century's nightmares? Hitler. The Depression. Holocaust. The Bomb. Iron Curtain. Cold War. And, after all of this, the United States a giant on the world's stage, a solitary superpower. We can't know his thoughts about these things, here in his unimaginable future, but we can ask ourselves, What would Theodore do? We can well imagine that he'd still see life in the world as a Great Adventure.

1919

Inventor **George B. Hansburg** *patents his pogo stick.*

Hugh Lofting *writes* The Story of Dr. Dolittle.

June 14 - 15 —
Englishmen **John Alcock** *and* **Arthur Whitten Brown** *make the first nonstop flight across the Atlantic Ocean, from Newfoundland to Ireland, in 16½ hours.*

June 28 —
The Treaty of Versailles is signed, ending the First World War.

More
Information

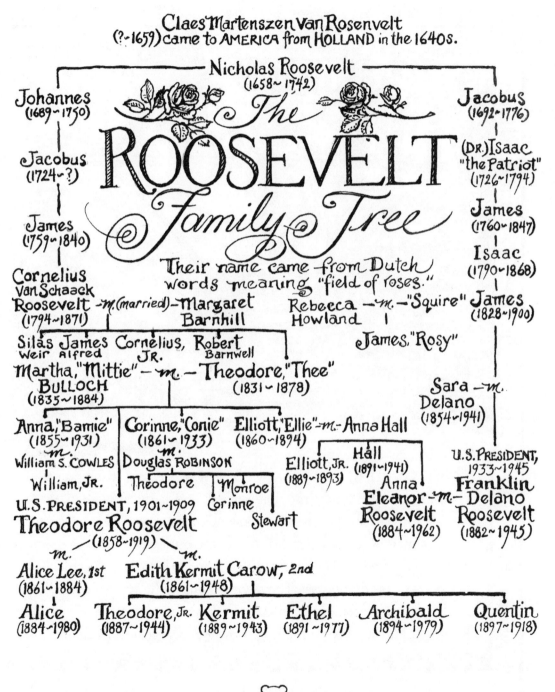

Claes Martenszen Van Rosenvelt
(?~1659) came to AMERICA from HOLLAND in the 1640s.

Nicholas Roosevelt
(1658~1742)

The ROOSEVELT *Family Tree*

Their name came from Dutch
words meaning "field of roses."

Johannes
(1689~1750)

Jacobus
(1724~?)

James
(1759~1840)

Cornelius
Van Schaack
Roosevelt —m.(married)—Margaret
(1794~1871)   Barnhill

Silas James Cornelius, Robert
Weir Alfred   JR.   Barnwell

Jacobus
(1692~1776)

(DR.) Isaac
"the Patriot"
(1726~1794)

James
(1760~1847)

Isaac
(1790~1868)

Rebecca —m.— "Squire" James
Howland   (1828~1900)

James, "Rosy"

Martha,"Mittie" — m. — Theodore,"Thee"
BULLOCH   (1831~1878)
(1835~1884)

Sara —m.
Delano
(1854~1941)

Anna,"Bamie"   Corinne,"Conie"   Elliott,"Ellie"—m.—Anna Hall
(1855~1931)   (1861~1933)   (1860~1894)

m.   m.
William S. COWLES   Douglas ROBINSON   Elliott, JR.   Hall
                                              (1889~1893)   (1891~1941)
William, JR.   Theodore   Monroe   Anna

U.S. PRESIDENT,
1933~1945

U.S. PRESIDENT, 1901~1909   Corinne   Eleanor—m.— Franklin
Theodore Roosevelt   Stewart   Roosevelt   Delano
      (1858~1919)   (1884~1962) Roosevelt
                                                                  (1882~1945)
m.   m.
Alice Lee, 1st   Edith Kermit Carow, 2nd
(1861~1884)   (1861~1948)

Alice   Theodore, JR. Kermit   Ethel   Archibald   Quentin
(1884~1980)   (1887~1944)   (1889~1943)   (1891~1977) (1894~1979) (1897~1918)

things beautiful, and horses and rifles and children and hard work and the

Sagamore Hill

SAGAMORE HILL

HUDSON RIVER

LONG ISLAND SOUND

NEW YORK CITY

OYSTER BAY

COLD SPRING HARBOR

0 2 4 6
miles

"At Sagamore Hill we love a great many things—birds and trees and books, and all

SAGAMORE HILL WAS A FARM AS WELL AS A HOME, and it took a small village to run it. Besides the maids, cook, and laundry woman, there was Mame Ledwith, the governess. Beyond the big house were homes for the gardener; farm manager; Mr. Amos, the butler; Mr. Lee, the coachman; and their wives. Local fellows were hired to help with the chickens, dairy cows, pigs, and horses. They worked out in the apple orchard, hay fields, and those planted with corn, barley, wheat, and rye. All of the Roosevelt kids worked in the huge flower-and-vegetable garden.

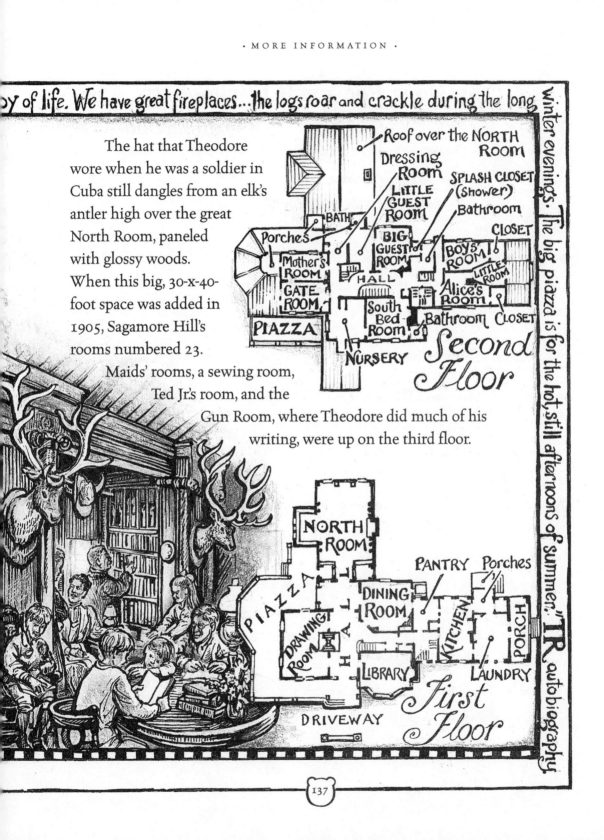

y of life. We have great fireplaces...the logs roar and crackle during the long

The hat that Theodore wore when he was a soldier in Cuba still dangles from an elk's antler high over the great North Room, paneled with glossy woods. When this big, 30-x-40-foot space was added in 1905, Sagamore Hill's rooms numbered 23.

Maids' rooms, a sewing room, Ted Jr.'s room, and the Gun Room, where Theodore did much of his writing, were up on the third floor.

Roof over the NORTH ROOM

Dressing Room

LITTLE GUEST ROOM

SPLASH CLOSET (shower)

Bathroom

CLOSET

BATH

Porches

BIG GUEST ROOM

BOYS' ROOM

LITTLE ROOM

Mother's ROOM

HALL

Alice's Room

GATE ROOM

South Bed Room

Bathroom CLOSET

PIAZZA

NURSERY

Second Floor

winter evenings. The big piazza is for the hot, still afternoons of summer." TR, autobiography.

NORTH ROOM

PANTRY Porches

PIAZZA

DINING ROOM

KITCHEN

PORCH

DRAWING ROOM

HALL

LIBRARY

LAUNDRY

DRIVEWAY

First Floor

Theodore Roosevelt Chronology

✳

Dec. 22, 1853 – Theodore (Thee) Roosevelt, Sr., and Martha (Mittie) Bulloch are married.

Jan. 18, 1855 – Their first child, Anna Roosevelt, is born.

Oct. 27, 1858 –Theodore Roosevelt, Jr. (TR) is born.

Feb. 28, 1860 – Elliott Roosevelt is born.

Sept. 27, 1861 – Corinne Roosevelt is born.

May 12, 1869 - May 25, 1870 – The Roosevelts travel to Europe.

Oct. 16, 1872 – The Roosevelts go to England, on to Europe, then Egypt and the Middle East. TR, Elliott, and Corinne study in Dresden, Germany.

Nov. 5, 1873 – The Roosevelt family returns to New York City to their new home at 6 West 57th Street.

1876 – TR begins his studies at Harvard College.

Feb. 9, 1878 – Stomach cancer kills Theodore Roosevelt, Sr.

1880 – TR begins writing his first book, a naval history of the War of 1812.

June 30, 1880 – TR graduates from Harvard.

Oct. 27, 1880 – TR and Alice Hathaway Lee are married.

Nov. 8, 1881 – TR is elected to NY state assembly.

Feb. 12, 1884 – Alice Lee Roosevelt is born.

Feb. 14, 1884 – 3 a.m. TR's mother, Mittie, dies of typhoid fever.

– 2 p.m. TR's wife, Alice, dies of kidney failure.

July, 1884 – TR begins building Elkhorn Ranch in the Dakota Badlands.

1885 – Work is completed on Sagamore Hill, Oyster Bay, NY.

Dec. 2, 1886 – TR and Edith Kermit Carow are married.

Sept. 13, 1887 – Their son Theodore "Ted" Roosevelt, Jr., is born.

April, 1889 – Pres. Benjamin Harrison appoints TR to the Civil Service Commission.

Oct. 10, 1889 – Kermit Roosevelt is born.

Aug. 13, 1891 – Ethel Carow Roosevelt is born.

April 9, 1894 – Archibald Bulloch Roosevelt is born.

Aug. 14, 1894 – Elliott Roosevelt, TR's brother, dies.

May 6, 1895 – TR begins work on the NYC Police Commission.

April 6, 1897 – President William McKinley appoints TR Assistant Secretary of the Navy.

Nov. 19, 1897 – Quentin Roosevelt is born.

April 25, 1898 – TR becomes Deputy Commander, 1st U.S. Volunteer Cavalry.

Jan. 2, 1899 – TR becomes Governor of NY.

Mar. 4, 1901 – TR becomes U.S. Vice President.

Sept. 6, 1901 – Leon Czolgosz shoots President McKinley.

Sept. 14, 1901 – President McKinley dies. TR becomes the 26th President.

Nov. 8, 1904 – TR is elected President in his own right

Mar. 4, 1909 – William Howard Taft becomes the 27th President.

Mar. 23, 1909 – June 18, 1910 – TR travels to Africa and Europe.

Aug. 7, 1912 – TR accepts the Progressive Party's nomination as candidate for President.

Nov. 5, 1912 – Woodrow Wilson is elected 28th President.

Oct. 4, 1913 – May 19, 1914 – TR travels in South America, along the *Río da Duvida* (River of Doubt).

July 14, 1918 – Quentin Roosevelt is shot down over France.

July 28, 1914 – Nov. 11, 1918 – The First World War is fought.

Jan. 6, 1919 – TR dies at Sagamore Hill.

Resources

BIBLIOGRAPHY

✳

Auchincloss, Louis, ed. *Theodore Roosevelt, Letters & Speeches.* New York: Library of America, 2004.

Bishop, Joseph Bucklin. *Theodore Roosevelt's Letters to his Children.* New York: Charles Scribner's Sons, 1919.

Collier, Peter with David Horowitz. *The Roosevelts, An American Saga.* New York: Simon & Schuster, 1994.

Brands, H. W. TR, *The Last Romantic.* New York: Basic Books, 1997.

Davidson, Donald J. *The Wisdom of Theodore Roosevelt.* New York: Citadel Press, 2003.

Lorant, Stefan. *The Life & Times of Theodore Roosevelt.* New York: Doubleday & Co., 1959.

Miller, Nathan. *Theodore Roosevelt, A Life.* New York: William Morrow & Co. 1992.

Morris, Edmund. *The Rise of Theodore Roosevelt.* New York: The Modern Library Edition, 2001.

Morris, Edmund. *Theodore Rex.* New York: Random House, 2001.

Roosevelt, Theodore. *An Autobiography.* New York: Charles Scribner's Sons. 1913.

RECOMMENDED FOR YOUNG READERS

✳

Blackwood, Gary L. *Rough Riding Reformer, Theodore Roosevelt.* New York: Benchmark Books, 1998.

Fritz, Jean. *Bully for You, Teddy Roosevelt!* New York: Penguin Putnam Books for Young Readers, 1991.

Harness, Cheryl. *Young Teddy Roosevelt.* Washington, D.C.: National Geographic, 1998.

Meltzer, Milton. *Theodore Roosevelt and His America.* New York: Franklin Watts, 1994.

Selda, Toby. *Simply "Father."* Sagamore Hill National Historic Site, 2006.

PLACES WELL WORTH VISITING

✳

Theodore Roosevelt Birthplace, National Historic Site, 28 East 20th Street, New York, NY 10003 ★ 212.260.1616

Theodore Roosevelt National Park, Medora, ND 58645 ★ 701.623.4466 ★ www.nps.gov/thro/tr ranch.htm

Sagamore Hill National Historic Site, 20 Sagamore Hill Road, Oyster Bay, NY 11771 ★ 516.922.4788 ★
www.nps.gov/sahi

www.theodoreroosevelt.org

The Pictures

The Roosevelts had no idea how helpful they were being when they had themselves photographed so often, but helpful they were and grateful am I. These photos and plenty of other reference materials helped me to visualize Theodore's world—the next best thing to being there. As many an artist did back then, I drew these images with a steel pen dipped in a bottle of India ink.

The Words

Could I have written more about how frontier America started morphing into a world power? Yup. But it is Theodore who grabs the lion's share of this book because, a century later, the story of a puny kid becoming a superstar, equally mighty in body, personality, and intellect, is still so cool. Much as George Washington embodied our revolutionary republic, TR totally stands for the way we were at the beginning of the 20th century. Thanks to the words of wonderful historians, including TR himself, I was able to tell his tale.

Acknowledgments & Dedication

Thanks to Ms. Betsy Polivy, Natalie Kinsey-Warnock (swell author) and I were able to see Sagamore Hill with our very own eyes. Thanks to the National Park Service staff and many other devoted people, folks can see Theodore's home substantially as it was when he lived there. To them all, this book is dedicated.

Index

Book design by David M. Seager. Design production by Ruthie Thompson, Thunderhill Graphics.
Text is set in Celestia Antiqua. Display type is Euphorigenic.

For information about special discounts for bulk purchases,
please contact National Geographic books Special Sales: ngspecsales@ngs.org.

Library of Congress Cataloging-in-Publication Data
Harness, Cheryl.
The remarkable, rough-riding life of Theodore Roosevelt and the rise of empire America /
painstakingly written and illustrated by Cheryl Harness.
p. cm.
Includes bibliographical references and index.
ISBN-13: 978-1-4263-0008-0 (hardcover)
ISBN-13: 978-1-4263-0009-7 (library)
1. Roosevelt, Theodore, 1858-1919--Juvenile literature. 2. Presidents--United States--Biography--Juvenile literature.
3. United States--Politics and government--1901-1909--Juvenile literature. 4. United States--Foreign relations--1901-1909--
Juvenile literature. 5. United States--Territorial expansion--Juvenile literature. I. Title.
E757 .H328
973.91'1092--dc22
[B]
2006029039

One of the world's largest nonprofit scientific and educational organizations, the National Geographic Society was founded in 1888 "for the increase and diffusion of geographic knowledge." Fulfilling this mission, the Society educates and inspires millions every day through its magazines, books, television programs, videos, maps and atlases, research grants, the National Geographic Bee, teacher workshops, and innovative classroom materials. The Society is supported through membership dues, charitable gifts, and income from the sale of its educational products. This support is vital to National Geographic's mission to increase global understanding and promote conservation of our planet through exploration, research, and education.

For more information, please call 1-800-NGS LINE (647-5463) or write to the following address:

NATIONAL GEOGRAPHIC SOCIETY
1145 17th Street N.W.
Washington, D.C. 20036-4688 U.S.A.
Visit the Society's Web site at www.nationalgeographic.com.

Printed in the United States of America